Un[illegible]g First Nations:

The Legacy of Canadian Colonialism

Dr. Ed Whitcomb

From Sea to Sea Enterprises
Ottawa, Canada
2019

Library and Archives Canada Cataloguing in Publication

Understanding First Nations: the legacy of Canadian colonialism / Ed Whitcomb

Whitcomb, Ed, author

Includes bibliographical references and index

Canadiana 20190190809 I ISBN 9780986596742 (softcover)

CSH: Native peoples – Canada – Social conditions. I LCSH: Indigenous peoples – Canada – Social conditions. I CSH: Native peoples – Canada – Government relations. I LCSH: Indigenous peoples – Canada – Government relations. I LCSH: Colonization – Social aspects – Canada. I LCSH: Canada – Race relations. I LCSH: Canada – Ethnic relations.

LCC E78.C2 W45 2019 I DDC 305.897/071-dc23

Publisher:

From Sea To Sea Enterprises, 2019
2130 Dutton Crescent,
Ottawa, Ontario, Canada, K1J 6K4

Printed in Canada by Lowe-Martin, Ottawa

Contents

Dedication

This book is dedicated to the tens of thousands of people who are working to end discrimination against Indigenous Canadians.

Preface: Understanding First Nations

Fifty years ago few non-Indigenous Canadians had any idea how badly First Nations had been treated over the previous century. In 1967, Canadians were celebrating the centenary of one of the greatest nations on earth, a land of freedom, equality, liberty, and prosperity, a model for the world. Those that did know the history of First Nations kept silent out of guilt, shame, fear of prosecution, complacency, or perhaps agreement with the policies and acceptance of the results.

Gradually the truth about Canadians' treatment of their First Nations began to seep out. The victims of the residential schools began to share their stories with their children, with others, with the public, and each courageous confession of suffering encouraged others to join in what became a gigantic bandwagon effect. The media started carrying more and more stories of other injustices, of higher-than-average rates of murder, family violence, drug abuse, incarceration, child adoption, poverty, and abuse of power by the police. Enquiries and studies documented what was increasingly seen as "colonialism," as the exploitation of one group by a majority and its government.

I was one of the vast majority who grew up ignorant of my people's treatment of First Nations. That was somewhat odd because I was always fascinated with them and their culture. I lived near the Dakota Sioux First Nations Reserve in western Manitoba. Seniors told stories about them and the area south of town was a traditional meeting place where farmers had picked up hundreds of arrow heads. The Brandon Residential School was a few miles to the east.

Like most kids I played "cowboys and Indians," but my sympathies were always with the latter, and I wore moccasins, made beadwork, could use a bow and arrow, hunted rabbits, and could place the major First Nations on a map of North America. I spent a holiday on the Sarcee Reserve near Calgary where my mother's cousin was the Indian Agent. His wife was Kootenay so my cousins are Métis. He talked about the way the Sarcee made decisions by consensus and always came up with the right decisions which were usually vetoed by the Department of Indian Affairs. He finally resigned in frustration. In Grade 7, I took the bus to Winnipeg to check out the collections of artifacts in the Hudson's Bay and Manitoba museums. The Grade 8 text for Canadian history described Louis Riel as a traitor - for some reason I reacted instinctively and wrote an essay arguing that he was a Father of Confederation.

History became my speciality at university, but the love affair with First Nations faded out of mind. That would place me in the mainstream of non-Indigenous Canadians for half a century. I remained sympathetic, noted articles about them in the newspapers, but did not focus on them. My careers centered on European History and the Foreign Service. As a diplomat I was somewhat aware of Canada's treatment of First Nations because diplomats raise human rights concerns with foreigners who sometimes point out that our record is far from stellar.

During my diplomatic career writing provincial history became a hobby, and by 2012 I had published short histories of all ten provinces and the North. Those were based on a decent knowledge of Canadian history, but there is hardly a mention of First Nations in the ones on central and eastern Canada after Confederation or the ones on the West after 1900. That is because Canadian historians did not include the history of First Nations in their histories of Canada after those dates. There were exceptions, of course, but today it is generally accepted that First Nations were largely left out of the history books and the media until their stories and grievances began to receive attention in the 1960s. This problem is far from being corrected but progress is being made.

The provincial books led logically to another project. All provinces have been treated differently by Ottawa, so the next book was a history of federalism. *Rivals for Power: Ottawa and the Provinces, the contentious history of the Canadian Federation* exposed an important myth dear to Canadians. We are not quite the law-abiding nation we think we are, because in its relations with the provinces, Ottawa has consistently violated the Constitution and the rule of law, and continues to do so with the support of a majority of Canadians.

While writing that book one of my friends, colleagues, fellow writers and political activists urged me repeatedly to write a book about First Nations. I repeatedly pointed out that there were lots of such books. But we gradually stumbled on a common theme between the book on federalism and the issue of First Nations: in both cases, the federal government has consistently violated the Constitution, treaties, the rule of law, the concept of fair treatment, and its own promises. So, in 2017 the concept of Understanding First Nations was born.

As expected, the information on Canada's treatment of its First Nations over the past 150 years was not difficult to find because, as I had told my friend, many books have been written on it along with numerous reports and thousands of articles. What shocked me was that I had no real idea how serious, numerous and deliberate the injustices had been. Although Canadians had been becoming more aware of problems for decades, a common theme in current literature is that they still do not grasp the full extent of the problems.

Many Canadians think the crimes committed in the residential schools were the exceptions; it is now clear that they were the norm. Many Canadians think the injustices are in the past; they continue to this day from coast to coast to coast. The Sixties Scoop did not end in the 1960s because the adoption of Indigenous children into non-Indigenous families continues today. Some Canadians do not accept that Canada was a colonial power but it was and still is. The myths that justified the policies are still alive and well in the minds of many Canadians.

So the concept of the book gradually emerged. It would be a short, easy-to-read, factual account of the problems facing First Nations over the past 150 years, many of which they still face. It would be "no-holds-barred," a clear account of what has been done to them by settlers and their federal government. It would be aimed at non-Indigenous Canadians who suspect things went terribly wrong in the past, suspect there are still major problems to address, and want a better understanding of the background and the current situation. It is not the history of the relations between Indigenous and Non-Indigenous Canadians or between Indigenous Canadians and the Canadian government because it is clearly focused on First Nations and their problems.

Several people helped with the preparation of this book. They include Clark Brownlee, Adrian de Hoag, Dr. Dan Livermore, Rev. Stan MacKay, Dr. James McKillip, Gar Pardy, Colin Robinson, and Paul Turcot. A special thanks to Glenn Cheriton of Commoners Books who did the layouts, designed the covers and was a fountain of advice on publishing and marketing. And to Ron Baron and Lowe Martin printing who did their usual superb job. Their hard work limited the number of errors of fact and exaggerations of opinion; remaining faults are entirely the responsibility of the author. And as with all my books, great thanks are due to my patient wife, Kai. She was raised in Bangkok, Thailand, so I have spent most of my adult life amongst visible minorities in Canada and often as a minority myself and have seen firsthand both tolerance and racism. That and a decade in Thailand, Indonesia and India probably helps me understand First Nations.

Introduction

"Too many Canadians know little or nothing about the deep historical roots of these conflicts. This lack of historical knowledge has serious consequences for First Nations, Inuit, and Métis peoples, and for Canada as a whole. In government...it makes for poor public policy decisions. In the public realm, it reinforces racist attitudes and fuels civic distrust.... Too many Canadians still do not know the history of Aboriginal peoples' contributions to Canada or understand that...we are all Treaty people. History plays an important role (and) to build for the future, Canadians must look to, and learn from, the past." (Summary of the Final Report of the Truth and Reconciliation Commission of Canada, p. 8.)

Of all the problems Canada faces, few are as important, complex or intransigent as the relationship between Indigenous and non-Indigenous Canadians. This sentence actually introduces the complexity rather nicely: the word "Indigenous" recently replaced "Aboriginal," which had come to represent three different groups of Canadians: "First Nations," "Inuit," and "Métis." First Nations is now the politically correct word for Indians, a group of nations like the Mohawks or Cree whom the government divided into about ten different categories such as Status and non-status and then sub-divided into 634 bands. The rest of the population are "non-Indigenous," though they have never called themselves that and are certainly not a single community.

In recent decades, Canadians have made progress in addressing the problems between Indigenous and non-Indigenous people. It is arguable whether that progress represented first steps or significant change, but a great deal certainly remains to be done. Half the people polled by Angus Reid in June 2018, thought the government was paying too much attention to Indigenous issues: nothing in this book supports those views. One essential ingredient of continued and accelerated progress is a better understanding of the problems faced by Indigenous peoples. This is not just "history," because many of these problems or their effects are still present and will be for decades.

The problems Indigenous people face were not simply created long ago by the French and the British. Discriminatory policies against Indigenous Canadians have continued to the present day under governments elected by immigrants who came after the French and British and those governments contained representatives of most immigrant groups. All non-Indigenous Canadians benefit from land taken from First Nations; all non-Indigenous Canadians are part of the problem and of the solutions.

The purpose of this book is to provide non-Indigenous Canadians with a short, easy-to-read, understandable and factual explanation of many of the problems that dominate what Prime Minister Justin Trudeau has called our most important relationship. This book attempts to "speak truth to power," and in Canada, power rests with non-Indigenous people and their governments. It is not a history of the relations between the two groups, an attempt to explain both sides; it is a history of how people who were here in 1600 have been affected and harmed by the "settlers" who came later, and how they have coped with those threats and continue to struggle with the consequences of non-Indigenous settlement and domination. An Environics poll conducted in July 2019 revealed that 89% of Indigenous youth and 87% of non-Indigenous youth believe that its very important for all non-Indigenous Canadians to know the history of how governments and society treated Indigenous people.

Numerous books, articles and reports point out that a major obstacle to addressing the problems First Nations face is the fact the many non-Indigenous Canadians have a poor or even false understanding of the history of the effects of settlers on First Nations. The lack of a proper understanding weakens the ability of governments and others to mobilize public support for solutions that could cost billions of dollars. This book is a response to those appeals for greater efforts to make this history more widely understood. There is some concern about non-Indigenous historians writing Indigenous history but in fact much excellent scholarship on these issues is produced by non-Indigenous scholars and this book draws on all of it regardless of the ethnicity of the authors.

Indeed, the potential readers of this book may well appreciate that the author is an "old white guy," one who has a Ph.D. in history, taught university, has written histories of all ten provinces and the North and a history of federalism, has published numerous articles on Canadian history and politics, is a political activist with a deep interest in human rights, and has tried to understand Indigenous issues from their perspective.

Another major problem in undertaking such a task is that the issues are so numerous, huge, and complex that a proper explanation of them suggests a very long, complicated, and detailed book. There are such books, and they are listed in the bibliography, but the "average non-Indigenous Canadian" who is interested in these issues is unlikely to read them.

How, then, to write a book on such complex issues that the "average non-Indigenous Canadian" might be tempted to read? The answer is simple: ruthlessly cut the subject down to size and recommend the books in the bibliography for those who want more detail. The first decision taken was to limit the scope of the book to First Nations, the people known officially as "Indians." There are dozens of such nations - the Mi'kmaq, Cree, Salish – divided into 634 bands living on over 2,000 reserves. They are divided into about ten different categories such as Status and non-Status Indians, and there are over 750,000 Status Indians and hundreds of thousands of non-Status ones in Canada. That still leaves an enormous amount of complexity, partly because while all First Nations have things in common, each nation has unique elements of culture, governance or situation.

Generalization is necessary, but over-generalization is misleading and accurate descriptions of differences would result in a very long book. The reader will judge how close this one comes to striking the right balance, but one must always bear in mind that there are great differences between the various First Nations. The great writer Thomas King said in *The Inconvenient Indian* that the drum was the only thing all First Nations had in common. That was an exaggeration but a good reminder of the enormous variations that of necessity are skimmed over in this short book.

The Inuit are a completely different nation with a very different history. Some of their problems are the same as those of the First Nations, some are different, and so are the solutions and the degrees of progress being made on their problems. The Métis are not included in this book. They are the descendants of the mixed marriages of First Nations and non-Indigenous Canadians, but only some of those Canadians are regarded as Métis. There is an historic Métis people, namely the descendants of white fur traders on the prairies, the people of the Riel Rebellion, but there are many others across Canada who call themselves Métis. Including the Inuit and Métis would require a much different and longer book, and those wanting to understand them will need to look elsewhere.

The second method of making this book manageable was to limit it essentially to background. It is designed to explain the problems First Nations face. It deals with the background, development, effects, attempted solutions, and current situation. It is, as the title indicates, a book about "*Understanding First Nations*." It is not a book about solving these problems because that would make it a very different and longer book. It would also make it infinitely complex because part of the problem today is that there is no firm agreement on solutions so a book about them would either promote some solutions or attempt to cover a variety of them.

Actually, the solutions have been known for over a century; the disagreements are over how to apply them. In the early 1880s, chiefs on the prairies identified a major problem, namely, that the government was not honouring its treaty obligations. The solution they proposed was that it honour the treaties. Simple as that! Ottawa never has, so that problem still exists, and that solution is still near the top of the list. Rooms could be filled with the reports of commissions, studies, submissions, proposals, research projects, and correspondence on solutions.

The 4,000 pages of the 1995 Report of the Royal Commission on Aboriginal Peoples contains 440 recommendations, mostly unfilled because the problem with solutions is that they have not been agreed upon, prioritized, funded, and implemented. The 94 Calls for Action of the Truth and Reconciliation Commission and the 231 Calls for Justice of the Inquiry into Missing and Murdered Indigenous Women and Girls probably cover most of the solutions to the problems left from 150 years of colonialism.

It is, however, impossible to describe the background to First Nations problems without mentioning to some degree the solutions they require, solutions others have proposed, ones attempted or partly or fully implemented. In describing issues such as child poverty, education, or infrastructure it will be pointed out that a large part of the problem is inadequate funding. Saying that clearly implies that a large part of the solution is increasing the funding to adequate levels. But such comments on "solutions" are meant to complete the description of the various issues, and there is no attempt here at a comprehensive analysis of what Canadians and their governments must do. The mystery is about why the solutions have not been implemented, why disgraceful situations have been allowed to continue decade after decade. That is what this book attempts to describe and explain.

The book is organized by subject rather than the more usual chronological approach to history. That is because the purpose is to *Understand First Nations'* problems, not their evolution or the evolution of their relations with non-Indigenous Canadians. Over a dozen major problems form the chapter subjects, issues like reserves, land claims, residential schools, incarceration rates, and child welfare. Each chapter is, to a considerable degree, a stand-alone essay on one subject. That inevitably creates a considerable degree of repetition, but that helps us *Understand First Nations*. An overall chronological context is still required to put everything in context, so Chapter 2 summarizes the entire history.

The problems facing First Nations were identified in 2004 by Special Rapporteur Rodolfe Stavenhagen, who was sent to Canada by the UN Commission on Human Rights. He found "poverty, infant mortality, unemployment, morbidity, suicide, criminal detention, children on welfare, women victims of abuse, child prostitution, are all much higher among aboriginal people than in other sectors of Canadian society, whereas education attainment, health standards, housing conditions, family income, access to economic opportunity and to social services are generally lower." He also found that Canada had been slow to implement the rights guaranteed in the Constitution of 1982. This book documents these issues, their causes, efforts to resolve them, and the current status.

The complexities are immediately apparent in the first chapter: "Who Defines Indians? White Men of Course." First Nations were never allowed to define themselves or their members as that role was taken by European governments and passed down to the Canadian government. It has left many Indians off the official list, which avoided paying them monies rightfully theirs. Canada has about ten different types of Indians and 634 First Nations bands. This situation served several colonial goals such as to divide and weaken the First Nations politically and deny them rights and funds. Part of the legacy is that while it is now recognized that self-government is essential, many bands are too small and financially weak to govern themselves effectively. Defining Indians thus becomes the first of many elements of an interlocking vicious circle in understanding the problems of First Nations.

The second chapter is a summary of the 400-year relationship between First Nations and settlers. It will not be further summarized here, but several points are important. Until around 1830, the relationship was quite positive. European powers and the colonists needed First Nations as allies in their wars and as partners in the fur trade. But First Nations were no longer needed after the War of 1812 and became, instead, obstacles to settlement. The relationship then became negative, and the settler community set out to "civilize" the First Nations and get them out of the way of settlement. Neither policy was entirely successful, and both have left legacies that explain much of the problems facing First Nations today.

White settlers and their governments created several myths about First Nations to justify domination, discrimination, government policies, and the theft of their land. This propaganda was extremely effective, and it is still believed by a considerable if not large portion of the population. That helps explain resistance to addressing problems. Seven myths are identified in Chapter 3: that First Nations were "savages" and that they suffered from four weaknesses - the inability to handle liquor, incompetence as adults, wastefulness, and laziness. A sixth myth is that Canada was not and is not a colonial power, and another is that the government "throws" money at them.

Sovereignty, or who owns Canada, is one of the most difficult issues and the subject of Chapter 4. Four European claims to sovereignty are explored: that the land was not permanently settled, that Europeans discovered it, that it was ceded by treaty, and that Europeans simply moved in and pushed the First Nations aside. These different theories lead to the current situation regarding land claims, un-ceded territory, and the complicated issue of self-government.

Chapter 5, "Treaties are for Breaking - by the Government" explains that First Nations had a long tradition of making treaties. Until around 1850, they were used to cement military alliances, obtain land in southern Ontario, open northern Ontario for development, or protect

First Nations from settlers. On the prairies, they were used to obtain First Nations acceptance of white settlement. The terms in these treaties were violated immediately and repeatedly and that continues to the present day. Most of BC was not covered by treaties and that is where most of the problems and negotiations are now centered.

Although the prairie treaties gave settlers control of 95% of the land, Chapter 6 explains how Ottawa almost immediately began whittling down that 5% and the value of what was left. Some land was not allocated at all. The land was to be of similar value so First Nations could become successful farmers, but settlers pressured Ottawa to move them to poorer land. Municipalities and companies expropriated reserve land. Ottawa has repeatedly attempted to turn communal land into private land so that it could be removed from the reserves and sold to non-Indians. On the other hand, it was and is almost impossible to expand a reserve. These are among the main causes of poverty today.

In 1876, Ottawa amalgamated several pieces of legislation into the Indian Act (Chapter 7). Ottawa gave itself control of almost every aspect of the lives of First Nations. It had no legal authority to do this as the First Nations had not been conquered, had never surrendered, had never accepted that they were subjects of Britain (Canada was still a British colony), and the treaties did not make them Canadian citizens or subjects. The Indian Act made them "wards" of the state, legally children with no rights. That is one reason why Canada is rightly defined as a colonial power and First Nations as colonized people. A series of amendments restricted their lives in almost every respect - movement, economic activity, drinking, dancing, cultural activities, voting, operating their own governments. It also gave them rights no other Canadians enjoy, and no one knows how to reform the Act to retain the rights and remove the wrongs.

Before contact (1600), First Nations throughout the Americas had various forms of government at the local, regional and international levels. Chapter 8 explains that these systems worked very well, better in some ways than European ones. In many, women had the vote and decisions were made by consensus. Europeans did not interfere with these governments when the First Nations were allies, but when they came to be seen as obstacles to settlement, their good governance became a problem. From then on, Ottawa used a variety of devices to undermine that governance. That was resisted, but gradually First Nations governance was severely weakened. Around 1950, First Nations began re-building their organizations at all levels, a process Ottawa resisted at first but gradually came to accept and has since been supporting. But Ottawa still "calls the shots" a lot of the time, and self-government is far from being restored. Canada is still a "colonial" power, First Nations are still "colonized."

One of the saddest chapters in Canadian history was the attempt to 'civilize" First Nations (Chapter 9). It began under the French and continued under the British, but the residential schools which existed before the 1850s failed. After Confederation, Ottawa decided to assimilate the First Nations and the chosen instrument was the failed residential school system. It was a disaster from the beginning, in every respect - sexual abuse, deaths, education, training, and its very purpose, "civilizing." Ottawa spent as little as possible and the schools were seriously underfunded until the last one was closed in 1996. Part of the damage has been dealt with through financial settlements, the Truth and Reconciliation Commission, and apologies; part of the damage will last for generations; and few of those responsible were held to account. The legacy of the residential schools is still part of the "unfinished business" that has to be understood and completed.

Before contact, there were no jails in the Americas; now Canadian jails are full of Indigenous people (Chapter 10). In 1600, First Nations had laws and rules and methods of enforcement, but imprisonment was not one of them. Jails, severe punishment, and solitary confinement were part of European culture. Few First Nations were imprisoned before 1850 when the systemic criminalization of their activities began. By 1900, they could be incarcerated for hunting, fishing, dancing, singing, drinking, giving gifts, travelling without permission, or wearing costumes and participating in rodeos or ceremonies without permission. Some of those laws have been eliminated since the 1940s, but the incarceration rate continued to rise mainly as a result of the effects of the residential schools, the degree to which Ottawa was successful in destroying culture, family structures and local governance, and the poverty that resulted from deliberate government policy. In 2017, 5% of the population was Indigenous but they made up almost 30% of prison population, statistics that suggest racial discrimination.

By the time Ottawa started closing the residential school system down in the 1950s, over half the students were there as welfare cases, and another crisis had descended on First Nations (Chapter 11). The explosion in welfare resulted from poverty and the breakdown of families. Provinces were responsible for welfare, and they began addressing the growing numbers by putting children up for adoption. This was the scandal of the Sixties Scoop, with some 20,000 children adopted into white families. The system was not designed to assimilate but was more effective than residential schools in doing so. It was strongly but unsuccessfully resisted by First Nations. Governments are only beginning to grapple with discrimination and other problems with Indigenous child welfare.

It has been known for decades that First Nations women have been murdered or gone missing and presumed to be murdered at a far higher rate than others (Chapter 12). This finally became a national issue in 2014 when the RCMP said the number was twice as high (1,200) as previously estimated. Demands grew for an inquiry. The Harper government refused but the new Liberal government promised one. It has been a near-perfect model of how not to do an inquiry: delayed implementation, confused and inadequate mandate, wrong Commissioner, low priority, short deadline, poor communications, interpersonal problems, resignations, failure to address key issues, and the appearance of politics. It has provided opportunities for the relatives of victims to gain closure. Its 231 Calls for Justice contain little that is new but should increase the pressure to address all the problems facing First Nations.

Infrastructure is a disaster on First Nations reserves, an oft-quoted fact being that Canada is in the top 12 on the UN quality of life index but if its reserves were a single nation, it would be #72. It is difficult to measure and compare roads, housing, or education, but water quality can be evaluated and statistics are kept. Chapter 13 looks at the issue of boil-water advisories on reserves, the causes, numbers, trends, problems measuring them, and the effects - poor health, depression, alcohol and drug abuse, the vicious circle all these situations feed into and reinforce. There is, of course, no excuse but the "excuses" are discussed (beaver dams!), and the current government's plan analyzed. The government has promised to fix the problem by 2021and good progress is being made, but, unsurprisingly, delays are being reported.

Chapter 14 covers non-residential schooling, health, and housing (roads and police are not discussed in the book). Before contact, First Nations had an excellent education system in terms of results. The systems imposed by settlers have never been good in terms of results. The main problems are serious underfunding, confused goals, and conflicts created by the goal of assimilation, but there has been major improvement over three decades and that trend continues. The section on health provides a series of examples of poor health services, inter-governmental squabbles over funding, and other problems. Housing is another disaster area that has received considerable media attention.

Chapter 15 points out that Ottawa has never acted as if it believed consultations were necessary with First Nations on issues that affected them. The best current example is the situation regarding approval for the Trans Mountain pipeline because First Nations were not properly consulted. The long history of non-consultations is recounted - the Indian Act, the transfer of natural resources to the provinces, Pierre Trudeau's White Paper, patriating the BNA. First Nations efforts to be consulted and reaction to being ignored are documented - the attempt to be involved in the constitutional talks, Section 35 of the Constitution, the rejection of the Meech Lake Accord, the current pipeline problems, and the meaning of "meaningful consultations."

The attempts by First Nations to regain control over their land, resources, lives and rights are recounted in Chapter 16. This includes the landmark cases like James Bay, failures like Oka, and the weakness in the process, and reasons for the huge backlog of cases. The major court cases are discussed: Nisga'a/Calder, Musqueaqm, Dalgamuukw, Tsilqot'in, Kahkewistahaw, cases that established rights to land, compensation, a degree of self-government, a voice in economic development, and some control over the environment. Section 35 of the Constitution guaranteed Aboriginal rights but did not identify them, and four conferences failed to do so. Court cases have filled in some of the gaps but there is an enormous difference between what First Nations want and what Ottawa and the provinces are willing to accept. In February 2018, PM Justin Trudeau promised to fix that before the 2019 election, but that will not happen.

The text ends with Chapter 17 on Reconciliation and Political Correctness. Canadians have erected statues and named buildings and other objects after their heroes, but some of these people are seen by

First Nations as the architects of colonialism. They have demanded that many statues be removed and that things be renamed. Many non-Indigenous Canadians have agreed, many have not, and historical revision, re-writing the past and political correctness have become issues in the debate over Truth and Reconciliation. Half a dozen famous Canadian names are in play, especially that of Sir John A. Macdonald. There is a real question of "political correctness," and since none of our heroes were perfect, where does the renaming stop? There are questions of politics, hypocrisy, symbolism and tokenism when some things are renamed or removed but others are not. Revisionism creates a backlash from the people whose support is needed for dealing with the real issues. The last sentence reads: "Perhaps rewriting history should be left to books like this."

Finally, a short chapter looks at past, present, and future.

A word on notes. This is not an academic study, and there are no footnotes for the thousands of facts and arguments presented here. The bibliography lists numerous scholarly works containing thousands of pages of notes. **A note on words.** One of the most difficult challenges in writing a book such as this is that words are used differently by Indigenous and non-Indigenous Canadians, and meanings change over time. This subject is often referred to as a "minefield," and such projects as being "fraught with pitfalls." One guide through the minefields is the 150-page *Elements of Indigenous Style* by Gregory Younging, another is recent scholarly works, and a third is the assistance of the readers listed in the Preface. But the purpose of language is to communicate with a specific audience, in this case, the average, interested, non-Indigenous Canadian. The words that matter to them are the ones they understand, not the latest term Indigenous Canadians or scholars are using. Those may be the current "politically correct" words, but scholars and First Nations are not the audience for this book.

Compromises were made with the use of words, and a few examples are important. Officially and legally, the subject of this book is *"Indians"* under the Indian Act, and that word is used when appropriate. For them, the term *"First Nations"* came into vogue in the 1970s and is used throughout the book to denote an individual, a band, or several bands. In the 1982 Constitution First Nations, Inuit and Métis were grouped together under the word *"Aboriginal,"* a word chosen by non-Indigenous drafters. That word has since been replaced largely by *"Indigenous" or "Indigenous Peoples"* meaning people who were here before colonization. It is used here when all three groups are being discussed. *"Non-Indigenous"* or "non-Indigenous Peoples" is everyone else, people sometimes referred to as settlers or newcomers.

"*Band*" is an inappropriate Indian Act word for the people who live on reserves, but it has come to be understood as those people and is used here. The words "tribe" and "native" are generally avoided. Settler names for First Nations are used eg. Huron rather than Wendat. The term "the federal government" is often replaced by the shorthand "Ottawa," and its Department of Indian Affairs is abbreviated as the DIA partly because its name has changed so many times.

Chapter 1

Who Defines "Indians?" White Men of course!

By the time Europeans arrived on the shores of North America they had evolved into several distinct nations, the Spanish, French, English, Dutch, and others. In North America they met several distinct nations, the Mi'kmaq, Mohawk, Huron, Cree and later the Sioux, Blackfoot, Haida, Salish and others. All nations meet a basic definition: they are a group of people with a common identity reflecting language, customs, beliefs, traditions, history and occupation of a specific territory who see themselves as being distinct from other groups of people. Using language as the main criteria, there were 86 Indian nations in 1600 in what became Canada.

The peoples of Europe, Asia and Africa were also named after their continents; the nations that inhabited the Americas were not, a fact that has caused confusion ever since and allowed the inhabitants of the United States to assume the name "Americans." When Columbus arrived in the Caribbean in 1492, he had no idea where he was, but he was aiming for the East Indies. When he saw brown-skinned people he called them Indians, and the Europeans who followed him used the same name. Officially, in Canada the descendants of the people the Europeans met are still known as Indians, and that incorrect name is a problem for them, for the government, and for everyone else.

The term "Indian" has several meanings, and the differences are extremely important. It is an ethnic description which applies to the descendants of all those people who came to Canada thousands of years ago or whose ancestors, by some interpretations, were always here. "Indian" is also a legal term applying to the people whom the government of Canada defines as Indian according to the Indian Act. Those people are "Status Indians," and are listed on the Indian Act's Registry, are registered with a band on a reserve, have the right to use reserve land, and have legal access to federal benefits. They are unique, and other Canadians do not have these rights. A separate category is "non-Status Indians," those who lost status, cannot establish it, or do not wish to establish it. Since it is a government definition, decisions as to who is and who is not an Indian have been made by non-Indigenous civil servants, not by Indians themselves. Indians are thus very different from all other non-Indigenous Canadians.

In the 1950s, Canadians began referring to Indians, the Inuit and the Métis as "Aboriginal," a term which was used in Section 35 of the 1982 Constitution. The three groups certainly do not see themselves as parts of a whole, and the term was increasingly seen as inappropriate. "Aboriginal" came to be replaced by "Indigenous," the word now used in the current title of the former Department of Indian Affairs (DIA). "Indigenous" refers to an inhabitant who was here at a certain time in contrast to those who came later, who are known as non-Indigenous, settlers, outsiders or newcomers. Officially, "Indigenous" refers to Indians, Inuit, and Métis.

Amongst the Aboriginal/Indigenous peoples, the ones who were Indians began to refer to themselves as First Nations in the 1970s to distinguish themselves from the Inuit, who are a separate nation and arrived centuries later, and the Métis, who could not have existed before Europeans fathered "mixed-blood" children. "First Nations" is an accurate and unique term because whether they came from Asia or originated here, they are nations and they were the first ones to inhabit the Americas. This book concerns the portion of the Canadian population that is, that could be, or that should be Indians according to the Indian Act, people now referred to as First Nations.

Britain ruled Canada after 1760 and in 1860 it transferred its Indian Department to the colonial government of the United Province of Canada (Upper and Lower Canada). That government had to define Indians and it did so as people living on a reserve who had Indian blood, were married to an Indian, or had been adopted by an Indian. From the beginning, then, the official definition was made by the white government, not by Indians, and it excluded many Indians but included people who were not. Those who qualified were officially "Status Indians," and their names and those of their descendants were listed on the Indian Registry.

At Confederation in 1867, the BNA Act gave responsibility for Indian affairs to the central or federal government, and in 1876 it amalgamated the various relevant pieces of legislation into the Indian Act. That Act regulated the relations between the Crown or government and various First Nations in central Canada and the Maritimes and identified some of their rights.

At first the government counted the people who were living on existing reserves in Ontario, Quebec, New Brunswick and Nova Scotia. As treaties were negotiated with the nations in northern Ontario, the prairies and the North, the names of the people whose chiefs signed those treaties were added. They became Status Indians, but they were also Treaty Indians and had rights not enjoyed by non-Treaty ones. Gradually most of the First Nations in Canada were recognized by the federal government and the names of their members were added to the government's lists making them, officially, Indians.

By the treaties, the First Nations ceded vast amounts of territory to the Crown and in return the Crown assumed financial obligations to them. That meant that the more names there were on the lists, the more money Ottawa would have to spend, and that gave the federal government a very strong incentive to limit the number of names. Since the government had little money and many priorities, limiting their number was a major policy goal from the beginning of the treaty-negotiating process. Limiting numbers remained a government policy until at least the 1980s and arguably remains so today. In the federal Cabinet, one minister was responsible for defending the interests of First Nations and often had other responsibilities which conflicted with those of First Nations. All the other ministers want federal money spent on other matters.

For at least a century, Ottawa used various policies to deliberately limit the number of names on the Registry, the number of Indians. In fact, it is more difficult to obtain an Indian Status card than a Canadian passport! The result was to deny rights and resources to hundreds of thousands of people, to define as non-status those who should have been Status Indians, to leave others defined as neither Status nor non-status Indians, and to make it impossible to know how many First Nations people there actually have been in Canada at any time including the present. These policies made Indians "disappear." One small example was excluding illegitimate children. Since Indians were regarded as a problem, making them disappear would solve "the problem," or so it was thought.

The first major policy to limit the number of names was avoiding the signing of treaties or postponing them as long as possible. The First Nations on the western plains knew in the 1870s that the buffalo were disappearing and that they were going to starve if they did not make agreements with the government. They were eager to sign treaties, but Ottawa ignored their requests until white settlers pressured it into making deals in order to facilitate the building of railways and open land for settlement.

Whole tribes were left out such as Alberta's Lubicon Lake Cree (from Treaty 8). They fought for over a century to be included and the fact that it took that long reflects the determination of the Department of Indian Affairs (DIA) to keep them off the Registry. When treaties were signed, the chiefs were asked how many people they represented, the people who would be registered and receive annuities from then on. The following year agents arrived with less money than required - Ottawa had made some members of the tribe "disappear." Some First Nations lived on both sides of the border with the United States. In Manitoba, Ottawa recognized the Dakota Sioux near Brandon as Canadian Indians but identified those near Portage la Prairie 125 km to the east as American refugees, an injustice that is currently being examined but remains unresolved.

Starvation was used to force people onto the reserves Ottawa had allocated to them and that certainly reduced the number of Indians. In the 1880s, some of the survivors renounced their status due to the conditions they were facing, and hundreds fled to the United States where they could obtain rations. This calls into question the deeply held myth that First Nations have always been treated better in Canada than in the United States. Many of them applied for "script" under a system known as the Half-Breed Script Commission, which also led to a decrease in reserve population. More "disappeared" Indians.

A major difference between European and Indigenous culture was that in many First Nations Indigenous women enjoyed far more status and power than did their European and later Canadian counterparts. When the federal government decided to assimilate and "civilize" First Nations, one policy was to impose male domination on their governments and societies. An important element of that policy was that a woman who married a white man lost her status as did her children, and she and her family had to leave the reserve.

Oddly, a white woman who married an Indian became a Status Indian and her children inherited their father's Indian status. Thus, a male Status Indian could marry a white woman who then became a Status Indian, but if his sister married his wife's white brother, she lost her status and had to leave the reserve. The children of both families were in effect Métis but some of these cousins were Status Indians and some were not and they might not be Métis either. At a family reunion several generations later some of the adults could legally have a beer while others could not, and some might have needed a pass signed by a white man to come to the event.

Some of these rules still exist, are still being challenged in courts, and are still difficult to understand or explain except that they reduce the amount of government expenditure on people who are entitled to it. Some forms of discrimination are inexplicable. Veterans who faced death defending Canada could lose their status for being absent from their reserve for over four years as did, of course, the hundreds who died making the world safe for democracy.

After the Second World War women of all colours began pressing for greater rights and addressing the discrimination in the Indian Act was one of their causes. In one of their first cases, Jeanette Lavell took the federal government to court in 1971 on the grounds that her loss of status violated the 1960 Bill of Rights. This led to a 1973 Supreme Court case with a 5-4 decision that the Indian Act superseded the Bill of Rights which was not legally-binding. The next case, that of Sandra Lovelace, went to the United Nations Human Rights Committee which agreed in 1981 that her loss of status through marriage violated her rights under the UN Covenant on Civil and Political Rights. That ruling was embarrassing but non-binding. In both cases male First Nations supported Ottawa because divide and conquer tactics work – by making Indian women unequal in the Indian Act, Ottawa gave Indian men a vested interest in keeping them unequal. Then Section 35 was added to the Canadian Constitution in 1982 and the government had to address the discrimination in the Indian Act. This it did, in part, with the 1985 Bill C-31.

By that very complicated piece of legislation, Indians who had lost their status by marriage (women) or enfranchisement (men or women) or whose ancestors or descendants had lost it, could now get it back, perhaps. Also, women could no longer gain status through marriage to a male Status Indian. One aspect of discrimination had ended but that presented a big problem. Reserves had been seriously underfunded and increasingly crowded for generations and the Status Indians living on them rightly feared an influx of new members even if those people or their ancestors had once lived there and were part of that nation or band. Rich bands might also have been reluctant to see their populations expand. Rather than address the underfunding problem which this would bring to a head, the government created a new type of Indian by separating, for the first time, status from band membership.

People who had lost their status and left the reserve could have their status reinstated by the federal government if a (probably white) civil servant accepted their application. But the bands were now given the authority to decide if they would also gain or regain membership in the band. Many reserves were financially incapable of doing that so most of the people involved regained their status but not their band membership. It was the latter that entitled them to live on reserves, share in reserve property and resources, and enjoy band privileges. Bill C-31 therefore continued to exclude some women and to reinstate some others but to a lesser status. It also meant that band councils and the Assembly of First Nations (AFN) still did not represent all Indians which weakened them politically. Those attempting to regain status faced the costs of travel, documentation, bureaucratic obstructionism, and possibly legal fees along with delays and stress and the possibility of ultimate failure.

Bill C-31 was more of "divide and conquer" politics, more symbolic than meaningful, a betrayal, a legally dubious gesture, and highly divisive in any First Nation whose "real" status members were now split between those who obtained band membership and those who did not. It ended some forms of discrimination and created others. By continuing to prevent Indian women from living on reserves, it maintained John A. Macdonald's policy of assimilation.

It was also difficult to regain status if marriage documents had been lost or destroyed. It could be costly if the documentation was weak and the government's lawyers were determined to limit the number of

Status Indians as they had been doing successfully since the 1880s. It was also of limited value if it did not carry band membership. It was also restricted: Indian women who regained status could pass it on if they married a Status Indian but if they married a non-status one, their children lost status. Some restrictions seem petty. To be registered, the child's birth certificate had to be signed by both parents. If the mother did not obtain the father's signature for whatever reason, the Indian child lost his/her Indian status. Non-Indigenous Canadian children do not lose their citizenship under such rules. So, the government continued to make Indians "disappear" only now it was the children of Indian women who married non-Indians rather than the women themselves. For them, the reinstatement of status lasted only one generation.

It was estimated that only 50,000 "disappeared" Indians would re-appear but that only about 10,000 of them would bother to apply. The government did not understand how emotional attachment to culture and status was. Within five years, 70,000 people had regained status creating a 19% increase in the number of Status Indians, and by 2000, 110,000 had regained status. Eventually 174,000 registered of whom 106,000 got status, and hundreds of outstanding legal cases reflected the chaos created by the half-measures. However, only about 7,000 of them had obtained band membership, the rest being the new class of non-band Status Indians. These numbers were an indication of how effective this policy had been in making Indians "disappear" between 1880 and 2000 and in saving the government money. The money saved helps explain the problem of poverty.

The government had made a half-step in the right direction, but women had still not achieved equality. That led to another court case, Descheneaux v. Canada, in 2015, and Ottawa was forced to make another attempt to end discrimination with Bill S-3. The draft legislation limited the correction to cases dating from 1951 but the Senate refused to accept that half measure. It demanded a more complete correction, the government reluctantly backed down, and the Bill passed in December 2017. Some of the amendments in Bill S-3 were implemented, some were subject to consultations between the government and First Nations. Those were completed in the spring of 2019 and the Bill came into effect in mid-August. According to the government, up to 450,000 people could regain status increasing the number of Status Indians from 750,000 to

1,150,000! It is not clear how many of them will become members of reserve bands, or what the overall financial implications will be for the government, the bands and the new Status Indians. There is still concern that women have still not achieved full equality, and it is still the government that defines "Indian."

On January 14, 2019, the UN Human Rights Committee issued a report stating that Canada's Indian Act still discriminated against women, and there is pressure to implement the new measures immediately. The report was based on a complaint by Sharon McIvor who argued that she still could not pass her Indian status to her grandchildren, but her brother could. The government had 160 days to respond and promised a report to Parliament in June.

The sad fact is that in 2019 Indian women do not have equality with Indian men because of a deliberate law designed to discriminate against them. It was passed in 1876 and has never been properly amended. Apparently, the remaining discriminatory rules could be eliminated by the current Cabinet implementing part of the 2017 Act by Order-in-Council. It has not done so, and the Inquiry into Missing and Murdered Indigenous Women and Girls has identified the sex discrimination in the Indian Act as one of the causes of the violence facing Indian women.

Another policy designed to make Indians "disappear" was Enfranchisement. In an Orwellian sense, the word also meant disenfranchisement. It was assumed that Indians would naturally aspire to advance from their alleged state of "savagery" to Victorian "civilization," which Englishmen believed to be the envy of the world. If they made the grade they would be "enfranchised" and bestowed the privileges of voting in elections, owning property and buying alcohol. They would also be disenfranchised from band council elections. To qualify, one had to be male, literate, free of debt, certified by a white person to be of good morale standing, have a university degree, or have qualified to join a profession such as law or the ministry. He would then cease to be a Status Indian and a member of the band. His wife and descendants would automatically lose status permanently whether they wished it or not. Intentionally or not, this policy would permanently undermine band leadership by removing well-educated candidates.

The band was to give the new Canadian citizen 20 hectares of land which he would own as private property ("in fee simple" or freehold tenure) and which he could therefore sell to anyone. That would remove the land from the reserve and some of those properties would eventually be owned by non-Indians. If all the adult males became enfranchised, both the reserve and all its families would "disappear." Whole bands could surrender status by majority vote, imposing enfranchisement on the minority, voting themselves out of existence. In 1958 the Michel Band in Alberta voluntarily enfranchised and its land was distributed amongst its members but in 1985 750 members regained Status. They also want their reserve reinstated but Ottawa says there is no provision in the Indian Act for that though they can be recognized as a new band. Ottawa could, of course, amend the Indian Act as it has done many times.

By 1876, only one Status Indian had accepted enfranchisement and his reserve refused to hand over the land. Again, the federal government had completely misjudged the commitment of First Nations to their culture and their people. By 1920, only 250 had opted for enfranchisement so the law was changed to allow DIA to decide that any male it deemed fit would be enfranchised. That was applied especially to veterans who were more difficult to dominate after serving in the war. Protests were ignored but though Enfranchisement remained a dismal failure, it was not abolished until 1985.

The cumulative result of these policies is that there are about ten different types of "Indians" in Canada today. There are Status Indians who are also Treaty Indians, Status Indians who are not, Status Indians living off reserve and enjoying fewer rights, non-status Indians, C-31 Indians who have both status and band membership, C-31 Indians who have status but not band membership, and unknown thousands of Canadians whose ancestors were here for over 12,000 years but have not made their way on to the federal government's lists or definitions of "Indians." Legally and politically, they are divided into male and female, and on-reserve and off-reserve ones.

The confusion is a daily problem for those seeking to regain status, those dealing with them, and land claims. After 24 years, a huge land deal has been agreed covering the area from Ottawa to North Bay, but there is a dispute over who can vote on it. The numbers range from 6,685 to 11,923, a good indication of the problems and inaccuracies in the Indian Registry. One rough estimate suggests that of the approximately 1.5 million Indigenous Canadians, 50% are Status Indians, 35% are non-status, 10% are Métis and 5% are Inuit. But no one knows how many Canadians of Indian descent are not being counted as Status or non-status Indians or how many Métis there are.

In January 2019, the First Nations Child and Family Caring Society took the question of Status and non-Status Indians to the Canadian Human Rights Tribunal. The issue was who qualified for assistance under the special policy known as "Jordan's Principle." On October 11, 2017, Minister Carolyn Bennett wrote all chiefs announcing that the government was initiating a review of Indian registration, band membership, and citizenship in consultation with them. Some female leaders asked how the question of whether women were equal to men could even be a matter for "consultations." Input was obtained up to March 31, 2018; an Advisory Panel was established in May; and it was to report to Parliament by June 2019. But as of March 2019, the government was still arguing before the Tribunal to limit the numbers eligible for assistance, that is, the number of Indians. Just as in 1870. It is still in charge of the process, still determining "Who is an Indian?"

The number of First Nations is also debatable. The Mi'kmaq are a nation in the cultural sense but were divided administratively into 27 First Nations or bands residing on 27 separate reserves in five provinces. There are seven Maliseet First Nations reserves, four Blackfoot, and so on. By the definition of nation used at the beginning of this chapter, there are dozens of First Nations in Canada, but if every band is a nation, then there are 634 living on over 2,000 reserves.

That is why the government divided the nations into many bands when the treaties were signed and why it has created almost ten kinds of Indian. The most basic tactic for empire-building and colonialism is the ancient policy of "divide and conquer." It has always been desirable for the federal government to deal with many types of Indian and hundreds of bands or First Nations. Ottawa and others can always say that they cannot meet First Nations demands because they cannot agree on what they want, or that it has met their demands as well as possible because some groups have agreed with some proposal. The politics of "divide and conquer" are evident daily in the debate over the approval of pipelines. These divisions of classification and nation/band/reserve are now a major part of the problem the federal government, First Nations and the rest of the Canadian population are trying to address.

Chapter 2

Some History (yawn)

"Too many Canadians know little or nothing about the deep historical roots of these conflicts. This lack of historical knowledge has serious consequences for First Nations, Inuit and Métis peoples, and for Canadians as a whole...History plays an important part in Reconciliation… To build for the future, Canadians must look to, and learn from, the past." (Summary of the Final Report of the Truth and Reconciliation Commission, page 8).

"Those who cannot remember the past are condemned to repeat it." (George Santayana).

There are serious problems facing Canada in the relationship between Indigenous and non-Indigenous Canadians. In 2016, Prime Minister Justin Trudeau said: "No relationship is more important to our government and to Canada than the one with Indigenous peoples." The problems are extremely complex, but as these quotations suggest, an essential ingredient in their solution is an understanding of their origins.

According to some views, Canada's First Nations always lived here. According to others, they came from Asia, moved down the east side of the Rockies between receding ice fields, and spread south, east and then north into much of the rest of Canada. The Inuit were a different nation who came later and settled in the North. An estimated half million First Nations lived in what they called Turtle Island and what is now Canada when Europeans started to show up on the east coast around 1600. If anyone owned the land in 1500, it was them, and whether they ever lost it is a matter of dispute.

An important aspect of First Nations culture was their attitude towards outsiders. They fought wars with rival nations, but outsiders were usually welcomed to their villages though practice naturally varied across the continent. Their openness reflected a fundamental attitude towards the land, that it ultimately belonged to the Creator and not them and was to be shared with others and not fenced off as private property. An important function of war parties was kidnapping men from other tribes to replace losses to warfare or disease. When the war party returned, one of the captives would be selected for torture and death, which was regarded as an honour. The others would be married to widows, adopted into their families, treated as equals, and given weapons and tools.

White settlers soon discovered this culture of hospitality. Missionaries were welcome unless they were viewed as threatening the villagers in which case they might be driven out or meet an unpleasant death. In the early years of settlement, French fur traders, the *coureurs des bois,* found life in the villages so pleasant that many of them took local wives and refused to return to their communities. This was so common that the loss of manpower became a problem in New France, and the inability to control young men weakened the authority of both the government and the church. There are cases of people being kidnapped by First Nations, then "rescued," and then returning voluntarily to the First Nations villages to the consternation of white settlers with their views of superiority. This situation produced an outpouring of propaganda from the Church which insisted that immorality rather than a happier life was drawing young men to the First Nations villages. That propaganda may still colour some current views of First Nations.

The first whites to wade ashore discovered that First Nations people were eager to trade and knew how to do it. Trade took place, words were exchanged, and relationships begun. French settlement along the St. Lawrence after 1608 produced little conflict because the tribes that Cartier had encountered in 1534 had left and the lowlands were vacant. In the Maritimes, the French settlers drained tidal flats, so their settlements created little conflict with the Mi'kmaq and Maliseet who retreated farther and farther into the forests. First Nations like the Huron had enemies and welcomed French assistance in their battles, so patterns of alliance were soon born. They rapidly extended to the wars between France and England for the domination of North America. These led in turn to numerous treaties between tribes and the European powers who discovered that the tribes had an ancient tradition of negotiating treaties and were quite expert at the process.

The main contact between the First Nations and Europeans was the fur trade. It provided much of the exports the colonies needed to pay for imports. The fur trade was based on partnerships between the companies and the First Nations peoples. The latter produced the furs and provided much of the manpower for the work along the routes into the interior. First Nations were excellent traders, knew the value of their products and those of the companies, and proved to be excellent customers, suppliers, and partners. In war and in economics, Europeans and First Nations peoples were natural partners and each respected the other.

After the British conquest of New France there was little contact between white settlers and First Nations in British North America except along the frontier. The settlements grew in the river valleys, the First Nations lived in the forests or to the north and west of settled areas. Contact in the fur trade was limited to the few white traders and the villages they visited along their route. Every year the canoe convoys of the fur traders would have passed through First Nations villages just twice. The traders would have met very few of the people whose furs they were acquiring. The French and English fought their wars alongside their First Nations allies who were often key to victory, but those wars were also fought along just a few waterways such as the Richelieu River.

Though there was little personal contact, official political relations were extremely important. First Nations allies were crucial to the armies of France and Britain as they struggled for supremacy over the continent. The European powers had much to offer - money, guns, food, goods, and support. Both sides had centuries-long traditions of negotiating treaties, and treaty-making was an extremely important prelude to all the wars between England, France, Holland, and later the United States. These treaties contained an important aspect of international law - governments make treaties with foreign entities, not with their own subjects.

In 1763, New France became a British colony. To reorganize its colonies, Britain issued the Royal Proclamation which remains one of the most important documents in Canadian history. It recognized the independence of the First Nations and their ownership of the land west of Quebec. But First Nations were outraged with wording that stated that France had "ceded" New France to Britain. One of their chiefs, Pontiac, pointed out that the land belonged to them and while Britain had conquered the French, it had not conquered them. Pontiac led a successful uprising against the British who were forced to negotiate because they could not afford another war.

Britain then sent William Johnson to turn the Proclamation into a treaty. He invited First Nations to Niagara and in 1764 over 20,000 came, representing 24 nations from the Atlantic to the prairies. There were days of ceremony, gift-giving and negotiations. On October 7, agreement was reached on the sharing of territory between two equal partners, the British Crown and the First Nations. The latter were not British subjects, and the French surrender of forts on the Great Lakes did not apply to the ownership of the land the forts stood on. The Treaty of Niagara has never been rescinded, re-negotiated, or over-ruled by Canadian law. Documents such as the British North America Act do not supersede it because it is a treaty between sovereign nations, and treaty rights are recognized in Section 35 of the Canadian Constitution.

Serious problems between First Nations and white settlers began in Upper Canada after the Napoleonic Wars when large numbers of immigrants began flooding in from Britain. The government bought tracts of land from the nations along the St. Lawrence and Great Lakes clearing what is now southern Ontario for settlement. By the 1830s, the attitude of the British and the colonialists had changed - First Nations peoples were no longer valued allies in war and essential partners in the fur trade but were now obstacles to settlement and expansion. They had become "inconvenient" and their ways of living were now seen as inappropriate. It was time to consider absorbing them into mainstream colonial society, to Christianize and civilize them, to assimilate them. This was not seen as a major problem because the advantages of civilization were presumably evident, and their population was rapidly declining due to disease.

This change in attitude developed slowly in mid-nineteenth century. A few residential schools were established through a partnership between government and the churches in which students were to be "civilized." The full flowering of the residential school system would have to await the acquisition of the prairies. In the meantime, Britain was withdrawing from North America, one aspect of which was turning its treaty and other responsibilities for First Nations peoples over to the increasingly powerful colonial governments. This marked another serious blow to First Nations because one of the essential roles of the British government since 1763 had been protecting them from white settlers and their local governments.

Another ominous development was that most of these decisions were made without consulting the people concerned. That established an unfortunate pattern that continues to this day. In all these developments and in the Indian Act of 1876, Ottawa was treating First Nations as subjects, taking on the role of parent and reducing them to the status of wards of the state, in effect, children. This was a violation of existing treaties, and subsequent treaties were a contradiction of the Indian Act because governments do not sign treaties with their own subjects. Ottawa, however, treated First Nations as though they were both foreign nations requiring treaty relationships and wards of the state requiring paternalistic supervision. First Nations never agreed to this situation and still do not, and the fundamental contradiction in Ottawa's relationship with its Indian nations/subjects has never been resolved.

One of the main goals of Confederation was to expand the new Dominion to the Pacific by acquiring the prairies from the British government and its local administrator, the Hudson's Bay Company and then enticing the colony of British Columbia to join. Failure to consult the people who lived on the prairies led to the Red River Resistance and the creation of the province of Manitoba. That development and the impossibility of conquering the First Nations due to the cost convinced the central government that it had to obtain the permission of First Nations to allow whites to settle on the prairies.

This required the negotiation of a series of treaties in which the First Nations "ceded" title to 95% of the land in return for reservations on the remaining 5% plus annuities, rights to hunting and fishing, and assistance in making the transition from a hunting to an agricultural economy. First Nations were willing to sign these treaties because they knew they had to make the transition, knew that white domination was inevitable, and because their numbers were rapidly declining due to disease and starvation.

For the First Nations, the treaties established permanent relationships and the sharing of the land. For the federal government they produced signatures on treaties allegedly ceding the land and allowing Ottawa to proceed to settle the prairies. Ottawa's subsequent actions indicate that it had no intention of honouring the treaties, and terms were broken from the day they were signed. First Nations protested as best they could short of open rebellion, but the decline of the buffalo herds, the arrival of white settlers, the overwhelming power of Ottawa, the example of the tragedy of the American Indian wars, disease, and the deliberate policy of starvation to impose domination left them no choice but to acquiesce. They were not always allocated the land promised, were moved from good to marginal land, parts of reserves were taken from them, and they slipped steadily into poverty. Their numbers declined until the 1920s when medicine began to address the diseases that were killing them.

First Nations wanted schools so they could become as educated as whites, but they wanted them on their reserves, the same as local non-Indigenous schools which were located within the communities they served. The treaties called for the provision of a school and teacher on each reserve. That promise conflicted with the growing desire to assimilate them and the assumption that the means to achieve that was to educate their children in residential schools far removed from their own families and culture. The promise of schools on reserves was therefore broken and Indian agents, missionaries, government officials, and the police began sending children to residential schools.

Such schools had existed for decades and had already proven to be failures. Nevertheless, the system was continued and expanded. When parents failed to respond, attendance was made compulsory and the RCMP kidnapped children and sent them to what were, in effect, child labour camps where they spent much of their time making the schools mainly self-sufficient. The system degenerated into physical and sexual abuse, did little to teach the students useful knowledge, skills or trades, weakened but did not destroy their culture, and left a legacy of enormous problems that Canada is still struggling to address. Every year the residential schools failed and every year the failed experiment was repeated, 150 consecutive years of failure.

For a century after Confederation, the federal government systematically pursued policies designed to make First Nations, treaties, reserves, promises, responsibilities, and obligations "disappear." The good land promised as reserves was not always provided. People who should have been counted as Indians and provided with benefits were left out.

Starvation was used to force acceptance of conditions that violated the treaties. Support for education and the transition to a European economy was not provided. Policies were adopted to undermine First Nations government, society, culture, and language. People were forbidden to leave reserves without permission. It became illegal for them to hire lawyers. It became increasingly difficult for them to pursue hunting and fishing as guaranteed in the treaties or to engage in other economic activities. Disease wracked their people and the residential schools weakened families and culture replacing them not with Christian civilization but with a culture of alcohol, physical and sexual abuse and a habit of lying to authority.

First Nations fought back against these policies as best they could, with different policies and degrees of success in the different regions. To a degree they did become successful farmers, ranchers, loggers, and workers. They passed down to future generations their recollections of exactly what had been promised orally to get them to sign the treaties. In many places they kept their language and culture alive and went to jail when caught doing it, in others they lost their languages. They engaged in passive resistance - no Indian agent could ensure that all members of his band were on the reserve, never participating in forbidden activities.

In some parts of Canada traditional forms of government were maintained beside imposed forms, elsewhere Ottawa was successful in severely weakening or destroying traditional government. Residential schools could not prevent students from running away or setting fire to the buildings. In the 1920s, band leaders started contacting each other more regularly. Provincial organizations began emerging especially in western Canada. Inter-provincial contacts became more frequent. Cutbacks to services during the Depression were a severe blow, but First Nations survived yet another crisis.

The Second World War marked a turning point and the changes it introduced are still playing out. Canadians who fought to free Europe from the Nazis found it increasingly difficult to justify the subjugation of First Nations in their own country, especially as Canada sought to project itself as an international champion of human rights. As in the Great War, First Nations volunteered in greater numbers than the Canadian average and distinguished themselves on the battlefield. Such veterans were not as easy to dominate. More students were acquiring better education, new leaders were emerging, and communications and travel were becoming cheaper and easier. Every year First Nations organizations grew stronger, larger, better financed, and better organized. Their demands became more articulate, targeted and pressing.

This new atmosphere led to the appointment of a Parliamentary Committee which held hearings from 1946 to 1948. Though First Nations had been sending letters and petitions to Queens and Kings, politicians and officials since Confederation, this was the first time they had appeared before MPs to give their views on the issues that affected them. The hearings publicized the plight of all Indigenous peoples. In 1951, amendments to the Indian Act removed some of the worst policies, but the overall goals and system remained unchanged. Assimilation was now to be achieved through encouragement rather than compulsion. Ottawa began phasing out the residential schools. It did not, however, change the way the remaining ones were administered or address the underfunding, so they remained a disaster until the last one was closed in 1996.

By the 1950s, these schools had become mainly orphanages, so their gradual elimination put an unsustainable burden on child welfare which was a provincial responsibility. To deal with that, provinces rapidly accelerated the rate of adoption of these wards. Since most First Nations were now living in poverty, the homes chosen were non-Indigenous, and the "Sixties Scoop" replaced residential schools as an instrument of assimilation only unlike the schools, the goal was not deliberate assimilation. At the same time, the federal government began to devolve the administration of various programs to the reserve bands and the power of the Indian agents declined accordingly. The bands did not have the power to change the programs and they remained seriously underfunded - some improvement but no real change.

More studies were completed such as the Hawthorne Report of the mid-1960s. It made clear that assimilation was not going to work and articulated the concept of "Citizen Plus" in which Status Indians were entitled to all the rights of other Canadians plus the special rights identified in the treaties. This was rejected by Prime Minister Pierre Trudeau. Interestingly, in the post-war period when Ottawa was underfunding its services to Indigenous Canadians at a rate of perhaps 2/3rds the amount the provinces were spending on non-Indigenous Canadians, Ottawa had such large budget surpluses that it began launching programs in provincial areas of responsibility provoking a half-century of political and constitutional crisis which almost led to the separation of Quebec.

In 1969, the federal government released a White Paper on its plans for the future of First Nations peoples. The goal of Prime Minister Pierre Trudeau and his Indian Affairs Minister, Jean Chrétien, was the same as that of Sir John A. Macdonald, namely the assimilation of First Nations into Canadian society and their "equality" with all other citizens. While Trudeau saw equality as a gain for many people, for First Nations it meant the loss of their status, their rights, their reserves, their identity, and most of the things they had gained in return for ceding most of their land to foreign settlers.

They were so outraged that the White Paper marked a turning point in the evolution of the First Nations movement. They organized to oppose it and forced the government to withdraw it, their first significant victory. That created momentum, confidence and the determination to see their rights codified and entrenched. It marked the beginning of a permanent and effective lobbying effort in government and media. The White Paper also backfired in the sense that many non-Indigenous Canadians came to recognize that First Nations were not disappearing and that they had rights which could not be taken away.

The issue of patriating the Constitution and including a Charter of Rights in it were of great importance to First Nations, but as usual they were not asked to participate in the process. This time they were not prepared to be ignored. Intense lobbying eventually led to the crucial addition to the Constitution of Section 35 which affirmed existing Aboriginal and treaty rights. They were not defined, and four subsequent meetings with federal and provincial politicians failed to define them.

These meetings took place under both Prime Ministers Pierre Trudeau and Brian Mulroney, but at Meech Lake Mulroney and the premiers reached agreement on Quebec's demands in a single day. First Nations were infuriated, and three years later a Cree MLA in Manitoba, Elijah Harper, refused consent to a continuation of the debate on the Meech Lake Accord, effectively killing it. First Nations were then invited to participate in the next round of constitutional talks in which they did achieve some of their demands. That agreement, the Charlottetown

Accord, failed to win approval but (male) First Nations leaders had established the right to participate in first ministers' meetings.

PM Mulroney fell back on one traditional governmental approach to problems by appointing a commission to examine the issues. This was timely because First Nations were running short of patience, as exemplified by the violent standoffs at Oka in 1990 and Gustafsen Lake and Ipperwash in 1995. The Royal Commission on Aboriginal Peoples (RCAP) went to work in 1991 and produced a massive report in 1995. It implied that Canada did, indeed, have a colonial past, but it did not acknowledge that current policies were still colonial. As with previous reports, its 440 recommendations were largely ignored, and Indigenous peoples fell further into poverty and despair.

By then Canadians were proud that their country always ranked in the UN's top 12 for quality of life, but if Indigenous peoples had formed their own country, it would have ranked 72nd. In 1995-6, the new government of Jean Chrétien balanced the federal budget in part with cuts to services to First Nations whose budget increases were then frozen at 2% annually. Later such limits were lifted on other budgets but were maintained on those of the DIA until 2016. The gap between services to Indigenous and non-Indigenous Canadians is now being closed but the damage of decades of underfunding will affect the entire country for generations.

In the absence of progress on the political front, First Nations continued to take their cases to the courts. There they encountered a change in attitude as judges began to accept that what First Nations had been promised orally was as legally binding as what government officials had recorded about the negotiations, that is, that oral history had to be accepted as evidence and given proper weight. As a result, First Nations won more and more court cases defining their rights, land claims and other issues.

That process continues to this day. In addition, in the past decade the survivors of residential schools have received apologies and financial compensation, the Truth and Reconciliation Commission has issued a massive report with 94 recommendations which the government has accepted but only partially implemented, a settlement of the Sixties Scoop scandal is underway, many land claims have been settled, more accurate history is being taught in the schools, and in June 2019 the Inquiry into

Missing and Murdered Indigenous Women and Girls issued a Report with 231 recommendations on how to address that tragedy. In as much as non-Indigenous Canadians are now learning their history, there is hope that Canada's First Nations will increasingly be treated as both equals and as having special rights stemming from the fact that they are sharing their land with the newcomers.

Chapter 3

Settler Myths About First Nations

One of the major problems underlying the relationship between Indigenous and non-Indigenous Canadians and the treatment of the former by the latter is a series of myths that have been created and perpetuated by the white settlers. This process began as soon as Europeans landed in the Americas and it has gone on ever since. Traces of it can still be found in the Canadian media, in books and literature, and in the views of those Canadians who do not know that what they think is reality is often myth.

This chapter examines seven common myths. One of the most important is that First Nations were "savages." Four other myths suggest that First Nations have physical, moral or character defects to which white Canadians are immune including the ability to consume liquor, incompetence as parents, wastefulness with money, and laziness. Such defects are found in people of all ethnic backgrounds and singling out such defects in one group is racism.

A more modern myth is that Canada was not and is not a colonial power. The 1876 Indian Act clearly gave Ottawa the same sort of control of First Nations as European powers exercised in their overseas colonies, and, unlike in Europe's former colonies, in Canada those powers are still in effect and still being enforced. A popular modern myth is that Ottawa "throws money" at First Nations. In fact, it has always underfunded them compared to what it and the provinces spend on non-Indigenous Canadians.

The first myth is that the people who lived in the Americas were "savages." Europeans had (and have) a superiority complex, the belief that their religion, Christianity, and their "liberal" and "modern" values and beliefs and ways of doing things were (and are) superior to those of any other race or group of nations. There was (and is) no factual basis for this arrogance, and Chinese, Arab and other civilizations had often been far superior to European ones in many respects. But the Europeans of 1600 certainly thought themselves to be God's chosen people and saw others as inferior, especially Africans and these newly discovered people in the Americas. The latter, accordingly, were viewed as "savages" in every way, in their religious beliefs, their personal relationships, their forms of government, their language and culture, their personal habits, and even in the food they ate. The latter myth cost Europeans dearly as they died clinging to their European diets in the cold Canadian winter while the healthy "savages" nearby tried to save them by providing food and nourishment that would have kept them alive.

There was never any truth to the myth of the "savage Indian." In 1600, First Nations people throughout the Americas had fully developed societies. They were not the same as European ones, but that did not make them inferior and in some ways they were superior. They had trading networks as large as the North American Free Trade area. They had treaties to manage relations between nations and amongst the confederacies. The Inca and Aztec Empires had sophisticated administrative, financial and communications systems. Their religious values and social norms were as well developed as European ones, their forms of government superior in some respects, and their health systems were based on a combination of extensive knowledge of the healing properties of plants and of the importance of psychology and spiritual comfort. Europeans were superior in many aspects of technology and learning, but not knowing how to write or make muskets did not make Indians "savages."

The myth of the "savage" pervaded European and Euro-Canadian thinking from contact until at least the late twentieth century and probably remains alive in the minds of some Canadians today. It underlined the reserve system, the residential schools, the adoption policy known as the Sixties Scoop, the underfunding of services to Indigenous peoples, and the racism that is still reflected in the police carding of innocent people, the high incarceration rates, the belief that Ottawa is "throwing" money at the reserves, and the failure to deal with missing and murdered women and children. At sporting events in Canada today, First Nations players are called "savages" by the parents of non-Indigenous players, and little is done to punish or correct that racist behaviour.

Another myth that emerged soon after contact was that of the "drunken Indian." Unlike the idea of "savagery," there was some evidence for this one. Dreams and their interpretation played a major role in the religion and life of many First Nations. Alcohol was not new to them, but brandy and rum were far more powerful than traditional products. First Nations discovered that consuming large quantities of the stronger types of alcohol enhanced their dreams, so some of them got drunk and enjoyed the wonderful visions that ensued. Missionaries were horrified and set out to deal with this unforeseen consequence of the fur trade. The problem was soon identified by the people themselves whose leaders have worked ever since to limit the supply of alcohol and drugs to their communities.

But white people also get drunk and have dreams, and the myth of the "drunken Indian" is the idea that unlike Europeans, First Nations peoples have a far lower physical tolerance for alcohol. This myth was debunked decades ago - First Nations metabolize alcohol at the same rate as Europeans. The myth is based on the incidence of drinking and on observation reinforced by racism. When minorities of any colour including whites get drunk in public, they are more likely to be noticed because they stand out, European tourists at Asian beach resorts providing a good example. An above-average number of First Nations are in the 16-30 age demographic, the one most prone to heavy drinking in all ethnic groups.

The policies pursued by the federal government produced a high incidence of poverty, violence and despair within First Nations society and are reflected in abuse of alcohol and drugs. The fact that it was illegal for First Nations people to drink before 1951 meant that when they obtained liquor, they consumed it quickly, the same as underage whites do to avoid being caught with the illegal substance. All this creates an image of people "unable to hold their liquor" when the drunkenness results from policies made by governments run by non-Indigenous Canadians. In fact, fewer First Nations drink alcohol than non-Indigenous Canadians but the ones who do are more likely to be noticed.

Similar to the myth of the "savage" is that of the "incompetent Indian." It would seem to settlers that if children were being raised as "savages," then their parents must have been incompetent, teaching them bad habits and instilling false beliefs. This was not good for the children and would perpetuate the division of Canada into two societies, the good "settler" one and the bad "savage" one. Around the 1830s, the idea emerged that First Nations should be assimilated into white society and become "brown Canadians" with all the good values and work habits of Christians. That required removing children from their "incompetent" parents, and the residential school system was developed. This policy continues today with the high incidence of seizure of newborn Indigenous babies by provincial welfare agencies.

A modern-day myth is that of the "wasteful Indian." The media regularly reports on money being squandered on reserves, on high salaries for leaders, on attempts by the federal government to force leaders to reveal salaries and expenses. Such articles lead to the argument that problems cannot be solved by "throwing more money" at the reserves because it will be "wasted." There is certainly waste in the management of funds, but that happens with all governments. Government waste is a problem of governance, not of the ethnicity of the people managing any administration.

Most governments in Canada are kept in check by systems that have been put in place to deal with human nature. Ottawa does not appear to have put effective systems in place when it devolved some degree of control to reserve councils. The idea that First Nations are wasteful defies their history. At the time of contact, it was European societies that were characterized by waste, one of the major differences between the two cultures. A main feature of tourism today is visiting the hundreds of castles and palaces of the kings and nobles who lived a life of leisure and extravagance. Europeans killed animals for sport, First Nations only killed what was needed for food and respected the dead animal's spirit.

Few myths are more baseless or damaging than that of the "lazy Indian." There is nothing lazy about Indigenous peoples and never has been. The myth was developed essentially to put the blame on them for their poverty. With that explanation, whites could avoid the truth about that dismal aspect of Canadian history and society, namely, that the poverty resulted from policies deliberately imposed by the federal government to save money and meet the demands of white settlers. The accounts of the wars and the fur trade identify people who could travel over great distances in short periods under difficult circumstances and without complaint. But after Confederation, a series of government policies gradually reduced them to poverty with the conditions that poverty produces in peoples of any ethnic background: malnutrition, poor health, disease, and unemployment, conditions that can be described as "laziness" by those unwilling to acknowledge the real causes.

The situation of the prairie people is instructive. By the 1880s, they knew the buffalo herds were disappearing and that they had to become farmers. They were ready and capable of making the transition. But unlike the settlers who began arriving from eastern Canada, they lacked the capital, equipment and knowledge necessary for farming. In the treaty negotiations they demanded government assistance with equipment, seed, animals, and instruction.

The government began reneging on the promised assistance almost immediately. Some reserves were carved out of good agricultural land, some were not, and First Nations assigned to poor land had no chance of ever being as good at agriculture as the white settlers. As the prairies were settled, the government forced them to move to reserves on marginal land. The instruction and equipment were inadequate for the needs of people who had never farmed. Seed was often of poor quality and sometimes delivered too late in the season. Still some of them became successful farmers and sold their crops on the local markets. This led to complaints of "unfair" competition from white farmers, so First Nations farmers were forbidden to sell on the local markets.

The ban on marketing was not entirely successful so the federal government reversed the policy of assisting them in the transition from hunting to a successful agricultural economy. It was decided that they should not compete at all with white farmers but should just have a "subsistence" agricultural economy in which they grew enough to feed themselves. They were provided with less technologically advanced tools. They were even prevented from buying agricultural equipment. As a result, by 1900 few had become successful farmers like the white settlers that were pouring into the prairies.

When the Spanish first arrived on the Pacific coast, they found rich and highly sophisticated peoples living in huge and elaborate houses, fishing in large ocean-going boats, and trading for goods over a vast area. That was still the case when in 1849 James Douglas arrived to establish a Hudson's Bay post in Victoria. The people there had most of what they wanted but they provided food, cut trees and built Fort Victoria in exchange for the few things the HBC had to offer that were new and valuable. There is no indication that they were "lazy," but they only worked when they wanted some blankets, pots or rifles. When they had what they wanted, they stopped working, and where they differed from whites was in the absence of greed and the European drive to accumulate more and more of everything.

As British Columbia developed, First Nations came to be engaged in all manner of labour in the white man's economy - fishing, canning, transportation, logging, dock work, mining, building roads and railways, and every aspect of urban employment including merchandising, construction, laundry, household staff, and prostitution. In as much as this can be measured, they appear to have been about as successful and rich as the immigrant population until about 1900. Then a steady decline into poverty began.

This decline occurred in every sector of the economy in which they were active. The best example was fishing. Beginning around 1900 federal and provincial laws and regulations steadily squeezed them out of that industry. Technology shifted to larger boats, but they could not obtain loans to buy them. Licences were increasingly given to non-Indigenous applicants. Traditional means of fishing on the rivers were forbidden and entire sections of rivers declared off limits. In the late nineteenth century, the canneries were major employers of First Nations, but a policy of discrimination led to the gradual elimination of that form of employment. They were squeezed out of other industries, logging, milling, mining, transportation. Then generous post-war welfare programs undermined the incentive to work and in the 1960s and 1970s, they rapidly descended into poverty, the result of deliberate government policy rather than genetic laziness.

A modern myth is the belief that Canada was not and is not a colonial power and First Nations are not a colonized people. Neither France nor Britain colonized and exploited First Nations the way they colonized Africans and Asians, and the relationships were nation-to-nation and governed by treaties. But as soon as the United Province of Canada gained responsible government, it began subjugating them. After Confederation, the Indian Act of 1876 gave Ottawa control of almost every aspect of First Nations affairs and Ottawa set out to destroy their culture and languages. By 1900 they were restricted in most aspects of everyday life. The elected band councils that are signing agreements with pipeline companies are creatures of the Indian Act, designed by Ottawa to replace hereditary chiefs and weaken First Nations governance. As long as that Act gives Ottawa power over First Nations, Canada will remain a colonial power. And as long as it is a colonial power, many of the problems facing both Indigenous and non-Indigenous Canadians will remain partly or wholly unsolved.

A favourite popular myth is that the federal government "throws" money at Indigenous peoples, problems, and reserves. One can hear and read this any time: "More money won't solve anything." "Throwing more money will only make things worse." "Money just encourages waste." "What about all those Chiefs making more than the Prime Minister?" The idea that Ottawa "throws" money at Indigenous people is not only incorrect but is the exact opposite of what has happened for the last 150 years.

Many of the problems facing Indigenous peoples are a direct result of the fact that the federal government has NOT spent money on them in the same proportion as it and the provinces have spent on non-Indigenous Canadians. DIA's large budget is sometimes quoted as proof of adequate spending – in 2013 one-third of it was spent on the bureaucracy, a huge incentive to maintain the status quo. It is difficult to square the idea that money has been thrown at reserves when 96 of Canada's 100 poorest communities are First Nations reserves.

One of the many examples of the difference between federal spending on non-Indigenous Canadians and First Nations concerns education. For the former, provinces and municipalities provided free, full-time education, paid teachers' salaries, and made Canadians one of the best-educated peoples on the globe. For the latter, Ottawa farmed out residential schools to churches while the students worked at least half the time to support the schools.

This penny-pinching was typical of all federal programs for First Nations in comparison to all provincial programs for non-Indigenous Canadians and makes a farce of the idea that Ottawa ever "threw money" at First Nations. After the First World War, First Nations veterans received smaller pensions than non-Indigenous ones. When the old-age pension was introduced in 1927, it did not apply to First Nations. The theory of waste is so prevalent that when the housing crisis on the Attawapiskat Reserve became a national media scandal in 2011Ottawa sent an audit team rather than housing experts, but the audit team found no mismanagement of funds.

After 1995, increases in the budget of DIA were capped at 2% per annum, an increase that accounted for inflation but not population growth. During the next two decades, Indigenous population grew by almost 30% so the per capita budget declined by 30%. As a result, money had to be transferred from capital spending to operations, so the quality of infrastructure declined. After the budget was balanced, transfers to the provinces for things like health increased rapidly but the 2% cap was maintained on DIA spending. More importantly, that rate of increase was based on a completely inadequate rate of expenditure in the past. The combined effect was a sharp increase in the gap between Canadian spending on First Nations and non-Indigenous Canadians after 1996. That period of shrinking relative expenditure is one of the main reasons for many of the problems First Nations face today, the ones documented throughout this book.

The 2016 budget began closing the gap between the amount the federal government spends on Indigenous peoples and the amount the three levels of governments spend on other Canadians, but as Chapter 11 demonstrates in terms of welfare, Ottawa has only begun moving in that direction, and only after being found guilty of violating the human rights of Indigenous peoples and shamed by United Nations reports. And it is not just a matter of "closing" the gap because the conditions of Indigenous people are far more serious than those of others due to fifteen decades of underfunding. Closing the gap in conditions will require far more funding than simply closing the gap in the amount spent per capita.

It will be very difficult for Canada to address the range of problems related to its First Nations peoples until these myths are excised from the minds of non-Indigenous Canadians. Given the prevalence of this propaganda over a century and the absence of correct information to counter it, that will not be an easy task. But it is well underway in schools and universities, the rewriting of textbooks and curricula, in literature, the arts, the media, and the controversies over the renaming of streets and the removal of statues.

Chapter 4

Sovereignty: the Creator or the Govenment?

O Canada! Our home **on** *native land!*

"Ottawa is built on un-ceded territory of the Algonquin Anishinabe Nation. The peoples of the Algonquin Anishinabe Nation have lived on this territory for millennia. Their culture and presence have nurtured and continue to nurture this land. I would like to honour the peoples and land of the Algonquin Anishinabe Nation. I would also like to honour all First Nations, Inuit and Métis peoples, their elders, their ancestors and their valuable past and present contributions to this land."

Official opening words for ceremonies in the City of Ottawa where the author's house stands on un-ceded land.

In 1534, a Huron explorer landed his canoe on the west coast of France and claimed the entire continent of Europe for his chief back in Canada. This might sound amusing if it were not for the fact that changing the names provides the basis for the Canadian government's claim for sovereignty over the territory of Canada. If the French had sovereignty over France in 1534, then by European definitions of the term First Nations must have had sovereignty over Canada, in which case it was not available for some European sailor to claim for his king. Sovereignty is a very tricky and extremely important issue.

Generations of Canadians have learned that Jacques Cartier sailed from France to the Gaspé Peninsula in Quebec, raised a wooden cross, and claimed the land in the name of the King of France. They also learned that the French were welcomed by the inhabitants and that trade took place immediately. But they might not have learned that those inhabitants objected strongly to Cartier raising that cross because they instinctively understood what he was doing, namely, laying claim to their land. Over the next decades and centuries, most First Nations across North America followed the same pattern in dealing with white intruders: they were welcome to trade, share the land and resources, hunt and fish, build trading posts and forts, and make settlements and villages. But First Nations never acknowledged that European kings and peoples gained sovereignty over the land.

First Nations could never surrender sovereignty over land because, in their view, they never had any such sovereignty. Although there were many variations, generally in First Nations religion, the Creator made the earth, water, air, and all the objects in or on it. They were just one of the objects living on the Creator's land the same as other animals. The Creator had sovereignty over everything, and they or other animals could no more have sovereignty over land than over sky, a lake or the ocean. First Nations owned their territories and fought wars with other nations for control of those territories, but sovereignty rested with the Creator. They built villages and homes and had trap lines which were theirs, but the land underneath the homes was owned communally not individually, and the right to a trap line did not bestow ownership of the land along it.

In Europe, in contrast, sovereignty and land ownership were well-developed legal concepts that were extremely important to the structure of the economy, society, and governance. The sovereignty of a ruler and of his country over any piece of territory was usually established by conquest and maintained by force. Gradually a system evolved in which territories were mapped out and described in treaties which identified which ruler was sovereign over which piece of Europe until the next war and subsequent treaty changed the borders and redefined each rulers' territorial sovereignty.

The French, however, did not conquer the inhabitants of the Maritimes or the St. Lawrence valley. The people they met were mainly forest dwellers and were not an obstacle to settlement; they were, instead, willing partners in war and the fur trade. France did not have to deal with the question of sovereignty between itself and the First Nations, but it did have to deal with sovereignty in terms of its relations with other European countries. As in Europe, the border between French and English "sovereignty" had to be established by treaty and identified on maps.

European laws on sovereignty were well developed. One was the Doctrine of Discovery. Accordingly, if an explorer employed by a European monarch came across land that no one else had ever seen, he could claim that land for his monarch. Cartier thus claimed to have "discovered" Gaspé and the Maritimes. He erected his cross to mark the discovery and the claim, and in European theory that made the King of France sovereign over that territory rather than the Kings of England or Spain.

The claim was nonsense because North America had been "discovered" thousands of years earlier, was known to Europeans because of the Viking voyages, and was obviously inhabited by the people Cartier was dealing with. The European myth of discovery was that land could only be discovered if the person discovering it was a European. The Doctrine was useful for European powers to divide up their "sovereignty" over the Americas, but it was pure fiction in terms of who had actually discovered the land and in 2012 the UN declared the theory to be racist.

Another theory in European law was the Doctrine of *terra nullius*, meaning unoccupied land. Accordingly, if land was not occupied, then anyone could claim it. Or, more accurately, if people did not occupy land the way Europeans did, that is in large agricultural societies, then the land was not "occupied" because Europeans saw occupation as permanent agricultural settlement and not nomadic hunting grounds. Europeans therefore declared that the First Nations did not grow crops, did not live in villages, and did not really "occupy land" because they migrated with the seasons or when agricultural land became exhausted.

However convenient, this was hardly an accurate description of either First Nations or European communities in the Americas. In 1541 Cartier described permanent villages where Quebec City and Montreal now stand. Aztec cities in Mexico rivalled the largest ones in Europe. The Huron and Iroquois had permanent villages, some numbering over 1.000 inhabitants. Europeans did not "permanently" occupy most of what they claimed sovereignty over - only a small fraction of the map of New France was settled by the French. Sending an explorer to the Rockies or the mouth of the Mississippi was the basis of the French claim to the central plains, and the English claimed the whole of Rupert's Land on the basis of a few forts on the shores of Hudson Bay. In short, almost all North America was *terra nullius* to the French and English, not to the First Nations.

A more solid case for European sovereignty was and remains the Doctrine of Occupation or Force. Essentially this meant that European settlers simply moved into lands in North America, cleared the forest and bush, built forts and villages, began farming, and spread out. When First Nations fought back, the Europeans defended themselves, survived, and expanded. First Nations were pushed farther and farther away, up the valleys, into the forests, and into more marginal economic space which explains much of their poverty today. This reflected superior technology and determination and eventually far greater numbers, but it was not the same as conquest and whether it transferred sovereignty is a matter of dispute.

That was how Europeans came to occupy Newfoundland, where all the Beothuks had died off by the mid-nineteenth century. Occupation was how the Maritimes, Quebec, much of eastern Ontario, and almost all of BC were taken over by Europeans. First Nations know that they can never regain control over these lands. Canadian sovereignty in these "occupied" areas is a *fait accompli*, but what First Nations can do, and are doing, is demand compensation for the loss of these un-ceded lands.

The question of sovereignty had to be addressed by the Europeans when Britain conquered New France in 1763. By the Treaty of Paris, France ceded to Great Britain sovereignty over the land it claimed in North America. As the British took the surrender of the French forts, First Nations allies of the French pointed out that the British had not conquered them, and while they would now control the French settlements and forts, but they did not now own the land underneath and around them.

The British government recognized the sovereignty of the First Nations west of Quebec in the Proclamation Act of 1763. To prevent trouble between them and settlers, the Proclamation stated that in this area First Nations could only sell land to the Crown and that such sales had to be done at a public meeting. White settlers could only buy land from the Crown, so the practice of settlers cheating First Nations out of their land would come to an end. The Proclamation is seen today as proof that the Crown (now the federal government) recognized First Nations sovereignty over all of Canada west of Quebec.

In the lands covered by the Proclamation, another method was developed to claim that sovereignty had been transferred from First Nations to Europeans and later the Canadian government. That was the "Doctrine of Cession," the use of treaties in which First Nations allegedly "ceded" specific tracts of land to the Crown. This process began after the American War of Independence when British Loyalists and their First Nations allies fled north from the United States. Land was available west of Quebec, so Britain negotiated treaties by which it purchased blocks of land and granted that land to the Loyalists including its First Nations allies. As logging and mining companies moved north of the settled areas in the 1840s, Britain negotiated the Robinson-Huron and Robinson-Superior treaties with First Nations opening those areas for development and settlement. On the west coast, HBC Governor James Douglas negotiated fourteen treaties on Vancouver Island in which Britain gained control of land in return for money.

The main series of treaties were the ones used to open the prairies to white settlement. White settlers could not simply occupy the prairies because there were too many First Nations there and conquering them was beyond the capacity of the new Dominion government. Ottawa therefore negotiated a series of treaties in which the various nations "ceded" 95% of their land in return for 5% that was reserved exclusively for their use plus other federal concessions.

In these treaties in Ontario, Vancouver Island, the prairies and later the North, the British and Canadian interpretation of the word "cede" was that First Nations had transferred "sovereignty" over the land to the Crown. But that was not their interpretation. As explained previously, in First Nations religion, the Creator is sovereign over everything, and the people on that land cannot transfer what is not theirs. What they believed they were ceding was the right of the Crown to allow whites to settle on the land and to farm or exploit it. They agreed to "share" the ownership of land, as they had been doing since Europeans first arrived, now with a formal treaty and defined boundaries. But to them, the Creator was still the ultimate sovereign over all of it and always would be.

The question of sovereignty over Canada's territory has never been settled and it may never be. The legal fictions of the Doctrine of Discovery and the Doctrine of *terra nullius* provide little comfort for the federal government. The treaties provide a better case for Canadian sovereignty over the portion of Canada that they cover and have the advantage that First Nations accept non-Indigenous use of the 95% of the land that was "ceded." The main problem with sovereignty is the fact that a large portion of Canadian territory was never ceded by treaty and the federal government's claim to sovereignty over it rests essentially on the Doctrine of Occupation. First Nations do not expect to recover this territory - settlers are here to stay and are in overwhelming control of Canada. But they expect compensation for the loss of territory they once clearly owned, the loss of which is a prime cause of their poverty, a loss that is an injustice that must be righted. One of the Calls for Justice of the Inquiry into Missing and Murdered Indigenous Women and Girls is for the government to officially renounce the doctrines of Discovery and terra nullius,

There are major unanswered questions about the ownership and sovereignty of those tracts of land and of some of the land that was "ceded" in signed treaties. These questions are the basis of hundreds of land claims, of billions of dollars in potential payments, of serious delays to projects for economic development, and of extremely complex negotiations and arrangements for compensation to First Nations who once owned, say, downtown Ottawa or Vancouver. They also ask that their rights be acknowledged by the phrase cited at the beginning of this chapter, something that is now gaining wide acceptance.

Chaper 5

Treaties are for Breaking - by the Government

First Nations had been negotiating treaties amongst each other for centuries before Europeans arrived in North America, treaties that covered trade, alliances, territory, and exchange of prisoners. The treaties were an oral tradition, which meant that the participants attached great importance to remembering exactly what had been agreed. Within nations some individuals were especially charged with remembering the texts of the agreements.

It was no problem for these nations to make treaties with Europeans. The two sides had different traditions regarding treaty-making, and they accepted some aspects of each others' ways. Europeans adopted the more elaborate ceremony, speech-making and gift-giving practices of First Nations and some of their use of language - "in perpetuity" became "as long as rivers flow." First Nations accepted that Europeans always made a written copy of what they understood had been agreed. One major difference, though, was that for First Nations, treaties were made in the presence of the Creator and therefore had to be honoured; in European and Canadian tradition treaties were honoured when it was convenient or unavoidable and were often signed with no intention of being implemented or honoured. The periods of peace between European powers in North America were, in effect, periods of violation and dispute over treaties until the two sides stumbled into the next war.

From the earliest contacts to around 1820 there were few problems with the nature of the treaties with First Nations. Most were designed to cement mutually beneficial alliances during the two centuries of warfare between England and France and later the United States. After conquering New France, the British government issued the Royal Proclamation of 1763 to organize its new territories. It was one of the most important documents governing the relations between the Canadian government and First Nations because it was a nation-to-nation treaty in which Britain acknowledged First Nations ownership of the land west of Quebec. After the War of American Independence, Loyalists fled north into British territory, and Britain negotiated several treaties with First Nations to acquire large tracts of land for the Loyalists. After the War of 1812, a huge wave of immigration from the British Isles led to several treaties and the surrender of more land in return for money.

By the 1830s, white settlers dominated the agricultural lands of Upper Canada, the First Nations population having either declined or been pushed northwards into the forests. The forests, however, contained valuable timber and mining resources, and companies moved in to exploit them. That produced conflict and the government stepped in to organize the territory. In 1850, William Robinson negotiated two major treaties: the Robinson-Huron Treaty and the Robinson-Superior Treaty created 21 reserves in the land north of the two lakes. First Nations ceded vast stretches of territory in return for annuities of four dollars a year, the areas specifically reserved for them, and the right to hunt and fish on the ceded land unless it was occupied and used by white settlers, loggers or miners.

While the value of the land ceded has risen exponentially since then, the $4.00 annuity remained unchanged. In 2017, 21 bands representing 30-40,000 people took the Canadian and Ontario governments to court claiming that the amount should have been increased. The case was heard in July 2018, and on December 21, the court agreed that the Crown had acted without honour. The judge stated that the treaties represented an on-going relationship and were not one-off transactions, and since the value of the ceded land had increased, so should the value of the annuities. Ontario appealed that decision, and negotiations are underway to arrive at a new amount for the annuities. If not successful, a judge will identify the amount. The financial consequences for First Nations across Canada could be enormous.

Treaties became especially important after Confederation. That scheme called for the Dominion to acquire all the land between Ontario and BC, land administered by the Hudson's Bay Company. Canada bought out the HBC's rights to Rupert's Land in 1869, but neither the British Crown nor the HBC owned or had sovereignty over the land. The First Nations had always been willing to share space with outsiders, but they were not prepared to be pushed aside by the waves of white settlers they knew were coming. They objected to the idea that the Dominion had "bought" the land from the HBC, saying that they should have been given the money since they owned it.

To the south, the Americans were conquering land from First Nations, but Canada could not afford a military campaign - the American budget for its wars was larger than the entire Dominion budget. Ottawa needed voluntary arrangements with the First Nations to clear the way for white settlement, and that could only be done by negotiating treaties. The First Nations were ready and indeed eager to sign treaties. They were well aware of the enormous changes that were descending on them: the end of the buffalo herds, declining employment with the HBC, the need to move from a hunting to an agricultural society, the relentless westward march of European settlement, and their diminishing numbers and strength due to disease. While Ottawa was in an increasingly powerful position, First Nations were still sufficiently numerous to block settlement and that gave them the power to make the best of a deteriorating situation.

Between 1871 and 1921, Ottawa and the First Nations negotiated the eleven "numbered treaties" covering what became the provinces of Manitoba, Saskatchewan, Alberta, northeastern BC, and much of the Northwest Territories. While there were differences, all these treaties followed a basic pattern reflecting what Ottawa was determined to achieve, subject to whatever the First Nations managed to extract in addition to Ottawa's opening offers. In these areas, white settlers would have access to 95% of the land, First Nations would retain 5%, the latter being reserves that Ottawa would identify in consultation with them.

Given the increasing imbalance in power and population, the 95-5 split was not unrealistic. While details varied between treaties, in general there was a one-time gift of $12 or $15 per person plus an annuity of $4-5 for every person and their descendants. There was provision for supplies such as ammunition and fishing gear, clothing, food, and blankets. Promises were made regarding education, health and welfare. The First Nations obtained support to transition from a hunting culture to agriculture with promises of agricultural equipment, livestock, seed, and training.

These treaties did not restrict First Nations to the reserves, and they could continue to hunt and fish on the land ceded until it was developed by settlers. Ottawa got what it wanted - the peaceful control of almost all the land on the prairies. The First Nations got what they wanted - the best deal possible, somewhat more than Ottawa had planned to provide. Both sides avoided the tragedy of the wars south of the border leaving Canadian history much less interesting than American. First Nations agreed to "behave" as good subjects of Her Majesty; they did not agree to be "subjects" of Her Majesty, a distinction that is extremely important. Altogether over 70 treaties were signed between 1700 and 1923.

The federal government began violating the numbered treaties literally before the ink was dry on the paper. In the First Nations tradition, a treaty consists of the things agreed on during the negotiations. When the negotiations were concluded, however, federal officials failed to include in the written texts some of the issues that had been agreed. In negotiating Treaty 1 in 1871 Lieutenant Governor Adam Archibald promised assistance with the transition to an agricultural economy but left that out of the text. When First Nations discovered the discrepancy, they demanded it be added. Four years later Ottawa agreed to provide the assistance but did not amend the document.

Ottawa promised to build a school on each reserve but violated that provision until the 1960s. It has underfunded the schools to the present day, a daily violation of the treaties. Ottawa took the narrowest possible interpretation of its obligations, one example being that it never increased the annuities from the original $4-5.00 even though the value of the lands surrendered rose exponentially over 150 years. For First Nations, treaties were always living documents governing an evolving relationship. The refusal to honour the letter and spirit of the treaties, the violation of the promise to look after the people in return for the land they ceded, is a principal reason for the poverty of First Nations. Some reserves were identified unilaterally by Ottawa, some were never even allocated.

On the other hand, the written treaties almost certainly included things the Chiefs had not accepted. The most important involved the issue of sovereignty. First Nations were prepared to share "ownership" of the prairies with white settlers, and that is what they believed they were doing. The Canadians thought they were acquiring "sovereignty", so when writing the text, they inserted wording that the land had been "ceded." There is no evidence such wording was used in the negotiations, and if it had been, and Ottawa's interpretation of it had been explained (ceding sovereignty), the Chiefs would almost certainly have refused to sign because in their view they could not cede the Creator's sovereignty.

Within less than a year, First Nations became aware that federal officials were not delivering all the things that had been agreed. When this was pointed out, the response was that those demands were not identified in the written treaty. When First Nations argued that the treaty did not then reflect what had been agreed, Ottawa's position was that only the written text had legal authority and anything else discussed or allegedly understood was irrelevant. When that interpretation was challenged in the courts, the courts upheld Ottawa's interpretation. That was no surprise as the courts were staffed with lawyers and judges steeped in British law which was based on the written rather than the spoken word. They were also, of course, staffed entirely by white people appointed by white governments elected by white settlers, analogous to one of two hockey teams setting the rules and selecting all the referees.

At the same time, First Nations discovered that things that had been agreed and written in the texts were also not being delivered, such as annuities, food, clothing, cattle, agricultural implements, and promises to provide services such as a school on each reserve. Various excuses were offered for the failure to honour the written text, but year after year Ottawa failed to deliver what had been promised. Within a few years of the signature of the first numbered treaties, unrest across the prairies was building up to a level that threatened a full-scale uprising.

For First Nations, however, giving their word before their Creator meant honouring the treaties, and with few individual exceptions they remained aloof from the 1885 Northwest Rebellion though their grievances were greater than those of the Métis and white settlers who did rebel. Nevertheless, Ottawa incorrectly assumed that 14 First Nations had joined the Rebellion and illegally withheld their annuities from 1885 to 1888. In February 2017 the Specific Claims Tribunal ordered Ottawa to pay them $4.5M in compensation.

For a century, the federal government insisted that the written text was the only thing that had legal meaning, and efforts to challenge that position failed. By the 1960s, however, things were changing. Young First Nations activists were emerging who supplemented their parents' determination and memory with law degrees and an understanding that their case could only be won on Ottawa's terms, that is, using Canadian law. They began using written documents with credibility in the white-man's legal systems to support the oral traditions of their ancestors.

Fortunately, such documents were available because the commissioners often left written reports of the day-to-day negotiations plus final reports of their work and translators often left notes on the discussions. Those records indicated exactly what the Chiefs had asked for, what the commissioners had agreed to, and what had been left out.

Over the last half century, the courts have repeatedly based decisions on both the written treaties, on these records, and on oral evidence, and First Nations have won significant victories to obtain what they were promised when they signed those treaties. These victories are discussed in Chapter 16 on land claims, a process that is far from completed as the federal government continues to fight its lengthy and expensive rear-guard action to avoid paying for the land it acquired in the treaties, the land which forms the basis of much of Canada's wealth.

While the courts have been forcing Ottawa to honour more and more treaty rights, the fact is that the federal government began violating treaties as soon as it signed them and it is still violating them on a daily basis. But such is the strength of propaganda and the weakness of Canadians' understanding of their own history that a 2018 Angus Reid poll indicated that 40% of Canadians believe the treaties have been respected!

The phrase "We are all Treaty People," has become popular. It is a reminder that anyone who buys property on land covered by a treaty is legally participating in the perpetuation of that treaty. In a sense it is a flawed statement in that technically it does not apply to people on un-ceded land; in a sense it is accurate, though, because the federal government has gradually extended many treaty rights to First Nations across Canada and, of course, non-Indigenous Canadians everywhere benefit from the land ceded in the treaties. History suggests that Canada will never be free of problems until its government honours its treaties, and Ottawa can never say convincingly that Canada is a country of the "rule of law" when it breaks the law thousands of times every day. It is as important for non-Indigenous peoples as for Indigenous ones to be able to say "We are all Treaty People."

Chapter 6

The Shrinking Reserve - What's mine is mine, what's yours is mine

"My land is my land. Your land is my land, From Bonavista, to Vancouver Island.
From the Arctic Circle to the Great Lake waters, This land was made for me alone." With apologies to First Nations, Woody Guthrie, and the Travellers.

The numbered treaties shared the western prairies between two groups of people: 95% of the land would be available for white settlement and 5% would be "reserved" for First Nations. At the time, First Nations outnumbered whites by a large margin, but a huge wave of migration was about to descend, and the First Nations knew that 5% was the most they could keep for themselves. With the guarantee of reserves and the other provisions agreed upon, they signed the treaties.

Judging by its actions, the federal government does not seem to have had any intention of reserving 5% of the prairie land for First Nations. As with other issues under negotiation, it made the minimum concessions necessary to obtain acquiescence to white settlement and immediately began violating the written and verbal promises that it had made. The promise to reserve 5% of the land was amongst the first to be violated. Interestingly, or perhaps not surprisingly, the government honoured its agreements to provide 5% of the land to the HBC and another 25 million acres to the CPR. Today in Canada's ten provinces, less than half of one per-cent of land is First Nations reserves, much of it marginal economically.

Several tactics were used to cheat First Nations out of their part of the bargain. The size of the reserves was to reflect the number of people in each tribe. The amount of land varied with different treaties but was generally around one square mile per family of five. The first tactic for reducing the size of the reserves was to identify fewer members in any given tribe than the actual number. In fact, large numbers were never counted as Status Indians under the Indian Act, so the federal government did not set aside land for them. Some nations were not included in the treaties negotiated in their territories. Alberta's Lubicon Lake Cree were left out of Treaty 8 because they were away hunting when it was negotiated! Some promised reserves were never allocated at all.

The reserve land was to be of similar quality to that which would be settled by whites. The stated goal of government policy was to help First Nations transition from a hunting society to a successful agricultural one, the same as whites, and that could only be done if they were allocated the same quality of land as whites. This was done to a certain extent and it succeeded in several cases. But farmers began to cast covetous eyes on those reserves, and pressure mounted on the government to move these populations somewhere else. The settlers brought with them their democratic political system including votes, organization, newspapers, pressure tactics, local government, friends in central Canada, allies in the police and courts, and influence on the politicians.

First Nations had none of these things. The government began re-locating them to reserves on marginal land. Resistance to these measures mounted and the government resorted to force and starvation. It worked and in the five years before the Northwest Rebellion the number of First Nations on the prairies dropped from 32,000 to 20,000 but they still did not join the Rebellion. Low productivity on marginal land was later used as an excuse to reduce the size of reserves.

After the 1890s, the government adopted the argument that First Nations were not entitled to retain land if they had not improved it. This condition applied to homesteaders, but it violated the treaties. Under this rule, the DIA transferred land to white settlers and used force when necessary to overcome opposition. In 1905, the Indian Act was amended to allow towns of over 8,000 population to relocate nearby reserves, and the Act was amended to allow companies and municipalities to expropriate reserve land for public works. On Vancouver Island, Governor James Douglas had established 14 reserves when the region was administered by the HBC, but a new Commissioner, Joseph Trutch, reduced the size of many of the reserves to make more land available for white settlement.

Some reserves were placed in forests, but forests were valuable for logging and perhaps sat on mineral deposits. Logging and mining companies put pressure on governments to allow them to exploit the resources in those reserves and governments found ways to allow them to do so. That took up some space. In some cases, the land remained part of the reserve, in others, parts were sliced off and the 5% allocated shrank a little more. These cases have been the subject of numerous court challenges and remain a major issue and obstacle to economic development today.

Naturally land had to be expropriated for railways and roads. First Nations fought to retain their land by whatever means possible – in 1923 the Iroquois Council asked the League of Nations to intervene to protect their land; one year later Ottawa abolished that band's Council. In 1918 Canada owed a great debt to its veterans – part of that was paid by giving them land on reserves while First Nations veterans received smaller pensions than non-Indigenous veterans.

For many whites, the goal of the Indian Act was the complete assimilation of First Nations into Euro-Canadian society, and the reserves were but a short-term expedient to bridge the transition. As more and more people made the jump from "savagery" to civilization, less and less land would have to be reserved for them. The transition to civilization was called "Enfranchisement," and if a male qualified, he would become a Canadian citizen. His band would give him 20 hectares of reserve land, which was now private property and could therefore be sold to anyone. Unfortunately, few saw much advantage in enfranchisement and nations refused to transfer land to those who did make the transition.

The word "Ipperwash" is symbolic of the shrinking reserve and of just how emotional and explosive this issue is for all Canadians. In both World Wars, First Nations had a higher rate of enlistment than the Canadian average and they distinguished themselves for bravery, toughness, and as snipers, and the use of Cree for military communications baffled the enemy. But the band at the Stony Point Reserve near Ipperwash at the southern tip of Lake Huron was not willing to also sacrifice its reserve which the Canadian Army wanted as a military base. Bad memories were still fresh, because in 1928 they had been pressured by the DIA to sell the lakefront part of the reserve to developers and in 1936 it had become Ipperwash Provincial Park. The band refused to surrender its land, so the government expropriated it, provided a cash settlement, moved the population to another reserve, and promised to return the land after the war.

The promise was broken on the very dubious grounds that the base was needed for training army cadets and Ottawa continued to use it into the 1990s. In May 1993, First Nations occupied part of the military base to force Ottawa to speed up negotiations. Nothing happened, tensions mounted, and the Ontario government sent the OPP and undercover officers to the nearby park in 1995. On September 4, First Nations activists entered the park.

Tensions continued to mount due to over-reaction by the police, the questionably use of helicopters, aggressive movements, miscommunications, misunderstandings, rumours, reports of firearms, and exaggerated statements by politicians. More police arrived and the police advanced on the occupiers. Anger and confusion arose, confrontations broke out, and Sergeant Ken Deans killed one of the protesters, Dudley George, for which he was convicted of criminal negligence in 1997.

In 2006, an inquiry identified numerous causes of the tragedy including the lack of training of OPP officers, poor management of the crisis by the OPP and the provincial government, possible racism, and the fact the federal government had not returned the land after the war as promised. It took another ten years to reach agreement between the Kettle and Stony Point First Nations and the federal and provincial governments to return the land, pay for repairing the environmental damage, and compensate the First Nations. Many members did not think the deal was adequate.

At the same time as reserves were being reduced in size or moved to less valuable land, unban municipalities underwent continuous expansion, often taking over valuable agricultural land. It was, on the other hand, almost impossible for a reserve to expand. Daniel Paul provides a rare example of a reserve that did manage to grow in his excellent book, *We Were Not the Savages*. The reserve near Yarmouth, NS, found its 20 acres insufficient to house a growing population.

There should have been no problem because a neighbour offered to sell 47 acres and Paul worked for the DIA. He helped obtain the agreement of the local and provincial governments and the local bank and did all the necessary paperwork. Senior officials in DIA then found so many problems with the transaction that it took seven years to finalize it. It is difficult to imagine that happening on the outskirts of any growing Canadian city. Fortunately, things have changed. On Cape Breton Island the Eskasoni Mi'kmaq First Nation purchased over 80 acres from two neighbours in 2017 apparently with few difficulties.

In the 1880s, it was assumed that Canada's First Nations population would disappear and there were good reasons for such a belief as their numbers had been declining since 1600. As Euro-Canadian and Euro-American settlement moved westward, nation after nation was devastated by disease. In addition, it was assumed that the few survivors would soon be assimilated - that was the job of the residential schools.

Given these assumptions about population there was little reason for government officials to concern themselves with the size of reserves or the commitment to set aside 5% of the prairies for them. The assumptions about demographics proved accurate for half a century as the population steadily fell. However, it bottomed out in the 1920s at around 100,000 and began a slow revival. After the Second World War, it began growing much faster than the Canadian average and now numbers over 750,000. The reserves, however, continued to shrink, and that, in addition to their location on marginal land, is one of the main causes of the poverty crisis facing First Nations today. The poverty results from 150 years of deliberate federal government policy and can only be addressed by deliberate federal policy. One is expanding the size of reserves which would actually cost little as many are on marginal land surrounded by Crown land. Here the problem is political or, as many believe, continued colonialism.

Chapter 7

The Indian Act: a Colonial Document

The Indian Act is one of the most controversial pieces of legislation in Canada today. It is a colonial relic from the distant past but every attempt to abolish it has failed. While the Canadian government does not and cannot question its legality, First Nations can and do. The French and British never conquered Canada's First Nations and the latter never signed treaties making themselves subjects of the French or British Crowns or of the Canadian federal government. But in 1876, Ottawa passed an Act giving itself control of the Dominion's First Nations and of almost all aspects of their lives. It implied that after over 12,000 years they were suddenly too immature to run their own affairs and were now wards of a paternalistic Canadian state, in effect, children. The state not only could make decisions for them but supposedly it had to, given their own incapacity as "savages" to look after themselves.

Accordingly, the Indian Act with its over two dozen amendments determined who was an Indian, where they could and could not live, how and where they could travel, how they would be governed, what they could own, buy or sell, how their funds would be spent, where they went to school, what they learned, what languages they could speak in public, what clothes they could wear off the reserves, what ceremonies they could participate in, what they could drink, and even the wording of their wills. The DIA and its Indian agents exercised enormous power over the people on the reserves and were almost certainly corrupted by the exercise of such power. That would help explain the century-long process of imposing more and more regulations on them as well as the last half century of resistance to transferring power from the DIA back to the First Nations. Many chapters of this book explore these issues in depth; this one will provide an overview of the Indian Act itself.

In the first two centuries after contact, various First Nations allied themselves with the French or English, but the European and First Nations communities lived quite separately. Economically they were partners in the fur trade but that produced little contact between them. After the War of 1812, however, First Nations were no longer of value to the British as military allies, Montreal was no longer a base for the fur trade, and their presence was an obstacle to white settlement. The relationship between Britain, its colonial governments, their white citizens, and First Nations changed dramatically, and those changes led to the Indian Act of 1876.

The Act brought together and expanded several pieces of legislation passed by the government of the Province of Canada (later Ontario and Quebec) before Confederation. They defined who would be protected, and ever since it has been the Canadian government rather than First Nations that defines who is and is not an "Indian." The Act applies to the 750,000 Status; it does not apply to non-status Indians, Inuit, or Métis.

Though the First Nations had never been conquered, in the early nineteenth century the British and Canadian authorities and the Canadian settlers decided that the they should become British subjects and citizens, that they should be assimilated into society, that they should abandon their languages, culture, economy, and way of life and adopt those of the Euro-Canadians. It is questionable whether the government had any legal basis for these policies, but it did have the power and it simply imposed them. That made Canada a colonial power and it still is.

In 1857, the government of the Province of Canada passed an Act to Encourage the Gradual Civilization of Indian Tribes. If people met certain criteria, they could become citizens with the same rights as white settlers at which time they would no longer be Indians. Males could then vote so the policy was known as "Enfranchisement." As Canadians they could also own land, so the reserve land they were living on would become theirs and cease to be part of the reserve. First Nations strenuously objected but their views were ignored by the British and Canadian governments. Three years later the Indian Lands Act effectively established the DIA. In 1869, another Act expanded the enfranchisement provisions to make more Indians disappear into the Canadian melting pot. In 1870, First Nations organized the Grand General Council to oppose these laws. Interestingly, the enfranchisement criteria made voting requirements for Indians more stringent than for whites - one would not want newly emerged savages to vote carelessly.

The Indian Act established that a "band" was a group of Indians who lived on a reserve which was a piece of land "owned" by the Queen. Indians had no choice in being identified as bands, but they never accepted that the Queen owned the land. The various nations were divided by the government into bands of which there are 634 today sub-divided into over 2,000 reserves. In contrast, the United States has roughly 300 bands. Those band Indians were listed by the government in the Indian Registry and they are Status Indians with rights and privileges. The reserves are held by Her Majesty for the use and benefit of the Indians on the band list. The DIA and its Indian agents can decide how any part of the reserve can be used for the benefit of those Indians.

The Indian Act contained a major assault on the way First Nations had governed themselves. In several ways their governance was superior to that of European states and that strength was a major obstacle to efforts to dominate and assimilate them. One goal of the Act was therefore to weaken traditional governance. It imposed European models with elected chiefs and councils and rules for the number of councillors, elections, time limits, and eligibility. These weakened the role of elders, traditional chiefs, and the vital importance of consensus, unity, and continuity. For decades, bands simply ignored these attempts, but that mattered little because real power on the reserve rested in the hands of the Indian agents, who chaired council meetings and could cast deciding votes, and of the DIA, which could remove councils and veto decisions. As bands reacted differently due to local circumstances, different systems evolved across the Dominion in terms of the relationship between elected and hereditary chiefs and their relative strengths and roles.

To prevent cooperation between bands, Ottawa introduced the Pass Law in 1885 requiring the permission of the agent to leave the reserve. The law was illegal, violated the treaties and the policy of assimilation, and required Indians to travel to the agent's house and wait for him to be available which could take days. Passes were first used in 1828 and the system was copied by South Africa in 1905. Indians needed a permit to buy groceries! A few hundred agents could not, of course, control tens of thousands of Indians, so the system led to indiscriminate and ineffective enforcement, problems between the agents and the First Nations, and disrespect for the law. Reserves and restrictions on movement and contact with settlers were, of course, a complete contradiction of the government's policy of assimilation – one or the other or both were bound to fail.

Section 88 of the Act introduced a significant wrinkle into governance by extending provincial laws to reserves. The First Nations' trustee, the federal government, had no say in the approval of provincial laws and First Nations could not vote for either level of government and therefore had no influence on any legislation. Ottawa had no incentive to support First Nations in disagreements with provinces because Ottawa always faced numerous problems with the provinces and hardly needed more. Instead of Ottawa taking the best example of any given provincial law and applying it to all reserves, it essentially abandoned whole fields of jurisdiction over First Nations to the provinces each of which could impose different laws. The numerous bands of Cree could then, for example, be subject to half a dozen different hunting laws. As late as 2001 the Auditor General's Report identified serious problems with this system including a lack of clarity, lack of First Nations input, confusion about federal funding, and the fact that programs were based on policy which was easily changed rather than legislation.

First Nations reserves were occupied communally, and individuals did not own the lots their houses stood on, a continuation of their ancient village system. But the Act contained the first of many attempts to turn the lots into private ownership partly to impose more of the European system, partly to facilitate the breakup of reserves and the transfer of land to settlers. For these reasons people resisted such attempts with considerable but not complete success. One negative effect of communal occupation was that people could not use their houses and lots as collateral to obtain mortgages or loans, but ways have since been found around this obstacle.

Several amendments permitted the shrinkage or complete disappearance of reserves. Reserves near cities of over 8,000 could be taken over (1905) and provinces, municipalities and corporations could expropriate reserve land for public works (1911). By the 1920s, First Nations were launching land claims, so Ottawa made it illegal for them to raise money to hire lawyers, effectively barring them from using the courts.

The Indian Act contained many examples of paternalism, of the government's self-proclaimed role as protector of people who were now relegated to the status of wards or children. Only Indians were allowed on reserves at night lest evil things happen. Liquor was not allowed on reserves at all. Children were sent away to residential schools to get a "proper" education. Parents were discouraged from visiting them. Adults needed permission to sell products (1881) or leave the reserve (1885) and in 1884 it became illegal to sell or give ammunition to Indians. Loopholes were gradually closed – in 1941 they needed permission to sell furs, something they had been doing since the first contact. Many of these rules were, of course, ignored and were unenforceable but that bred a habit of disrespect for the law, the government, the police and the courts.

The 1876 Act and its amendments had the very deliberate goal of destroying their culture. In 1884, the prairie Sun Dance was banned. In 1885, the west coast Potlach was banned. It was a ceremony for weddings and other occasions and the law was also designed to harass people and undermine traditional governance. After 1888 the Pass Law could be used to prevent attendance at ceremonies on other reserves. Artifacts were seized illegally and sold - First Nations are still fighting governments and museums to get them back. After 1914, one needed permission to appear off reserve in traditional costume or to attend stampedes, rodeos, and ceremonies. School children were severely punished for speaking their own languages.

The Second World War ushered in a new phase to the evolution of the Indian Act. Before it was passed in 1876, the government had followed a policy of assimilation without coercion. Under the Act assimilation was forced on people by a series of policies. But the Second World War was fought in the name of freedom and the liberation of Europe revealed the horrors of the Nazi genocide and the massive human rights violations throughout the continent.

Canada's First Nations had a higher enlistment rate than the Canadian average, had earned the respect of their comrades, and were not likely to go quietly back to their lives as colonial subjects on segregated reserves. Some Canadians realized that the cultural genocide they had been practicing against First Nations people was unacceptable, especially for a country that was championing human rights at the new United Nations.

In the late 1940s, a Joint Parliamentary Committee studied the Indian Act and the condition of First Nations, and Ottawa made several significant changes to the Act in 1951. It reduced its own control over the band councils, ended the ban on ceremonies like the Potlach, allowed councils to raise money and hire lawyers, allowed people to enter pool halls and sell cattle, allowed women to vote in council elections, and allowed people to wear traditional dress off reserve without requiring the agent's permission. But the amendments also strengthened provincial control over First Nations and the reforms did not end the policy of assimilation. Piecemeal reforms continued: in 1961 they could vote without having to give up their Indian status, a change which also ended compulsory enfranchisement. In 1985, the policy of enfranchisement was finally abolished and women who married non-Indians could regain Indian status under certain conditions.

After 1985, there were no major changes to the Indian Act, but several laws have been passed to address some of the problems the Act created. One change made it easier for people to establish a business when they cannot own property and therefore lack assets as collateral for a mortgage or bank loan. These efforts have continued with, for example, the 2019 budget providing $150M to support businesses. While some sort of consultations now take place, the government and its DIA continue to operate on the assumption that they know best.

An important exception was the passage of Bill S-3 in 2018 which restored status to some women. But the issue will not go away, and in February 2019, Quebec Native Women demanded that the Indian Act be abolished because it still did not give women equality with men. They argued that every time women had won a court case, the government had only done the minimum to move towards implementing it. That, in 2019, was still the reality and, in effect, the goal of the 1876 Indian Act - assimilation - has never changed.

The fact is that the Indian Act with all its flaws and negative historic connotations documents rights and privileges and status that are unique to Status Indians. It sets them apart from other Canadians, reflects the treaties, guarantees them a homeland that is safe from settlers, and holds out the promise of self-government. Despite the terrible conditions, First Nations have been able to retain their culture and some of their languages because they lived on reserves. They have no intention of surrendering the rights which they always had, never lost through conquest, or retained in exchange for the surrender of most of the territory they once owned and occupied. No one has figured out how to untie the Gordian Knot to retain what is valuable in the Indian Act while jettisoning what is not.

Chapter 8

Governance: Good, Bad or Problematic?

At the time of contact with Europeans, the First Nations in what would become Canada had three levels of governance, local, regional, and international. Local or village governance followed rules that were understood; regional and international governance was regulated by treaties. These systems had existed for centuries and applied to local tribes, to nations such as the Ojibwa or Cree, and to confederacies such as the Blackfoot nations. These systems of government often worked as well as or better than their equivalents in Europe. Naturally there were great variations from nation to nation across the continent, but there were also similarities that distinguished their forms of governance from those of the Europeans which also varied enormously across that continent.

Villages were usually governed by a chief or chiefs and a council. In some villages the chiefs were hereditary, in others they were elected, and there were many variations from nation to nation and even from tribe to tribe within nations. Where there were elections, all adults had a say, centuries before there was universal suffrage in Europe or the Dominion of Canada. In many nations that suffrage included women. Elections were organized by consensus amongst all adults, not voting, a practice that creates winners and losers. The old chief's son or a leader of hunting or war parties might have an advantage but did not necessarily emerge as the new chief. A chief who failed at his tasks would probably be replaced.

Decisions were usually made by consensus, and an issue would be discussed until all those who wanted to speak had done so and common agreement emerged. In these discussions the views of the elders carried more weight as it was assumed that they had gained wisdom from life's experiences. The views of chiefs and councillors would likely carry more weight, but they might not dominate. The opinions of women were important - men handled hunting and warfare but in village life, women's roles were more important than those of men.

Chiefs were not particularly powerful within their societies. Their job was more that of ensuring that consensus was achieved, that decisions were enforced, that food was properly distributed, that disputes were settled. Unlike European leaders, they had little power of discipline. The village chief might not be the best candidate to lead a war party so another man could be selected by consensus. During the campaign he would likely have more power than a village chief, but after the war he would revert to his previous position.

Because decision making was by consensus, the results were accepted by the community - whether to move to a new location, when to launch a hunt, whether to form an alliance. Traditions were understood and followed. Children were taught laws, rules, traditions, and adult roles by example, story telling, songs, copying adults, and playing games. As they matured, they eased into their roles in government, as members of the community, councillors, chiefs, or heads of war parties. Discipline was light and there were no jails, but serious crime was punished by death or exile. As an example, rape was rare but when it did occur, the rapist was so severely humiliated in front of the whole village that he and others were unlikely to repeat the offence. In contrast, Canadian law enforcement is so ineffective that most cases are never reported, few of those lead to convictions, and imprisonment produces hardened criminals.

At the regional and international level, some nations had organized confederacies. In the Maritimes, the Mi'kmaq nation had seven sub-divisions and a grand council composed of the seven chiefs. Another was the five-nation Iroquois Confederacy which had village, tribal and inter-tribal councils and a grand council of 50 chiefs which had been in existence for centuries by 1600. Its structure is the oldest participatory democracy in the world and was used as a model in the drafting of the American Constitution.

For 200 years the French and English made no attempts to interfere with the governance of First Nations. The European powers wanted strong allies in their wars and the quality of First Nations governance was a major advantage to the Europeans. The end of the centuries of warfare in 1814 completely reversed that situation. By the 1830s, First

Nations were no longer needed as allies or as partners in the fur trade and had become, instead, obstacles to white settlement. Now the quality of their governments was a problem for white settlers and their colonial governments and undermining those governments became a major objective.

The Indian Act contained a series of measures designed to weaken the capacity of First Nations to govern themselves. The most important element was the fact that the Indian Act effectively transferred power from the chiefs and councils to the government of Canada, the DIA, and their Indian agents on each reserve. The DIA then used its power, money, supplies, jobs, and favours to render First Nations governance virtually meaningless. There does not seem to be any constitutional or legal basis for this "colonization" of Canada's First Nations. Ottawa simply had the power to take control of their governments and their lives and it did so. On the reserves, Ottawa's power was wielded by the Indian agent. He and not the chief or council made the major decisions. Agents were, in effect, mayor, administrator, police officer, judge, jury, and enforcer, a set of roles no single person would be entrusted with in white society.

After the Dominion gained control of the prairies in 1869 it settled the First Nations on dozens of small reserves, each with a chief, each of whom could be played off against the other chiefs from the same nation. The reserves were deliberately separated geographically to reduce contact and cooperation. People saw through the policy and resisted it, demanding to remain united on larger reserves or to have the reserves close to each other. That was refused and resistance to it was broken by withholding rations until chiefs had no option but to move their starving people to the smaller, distant reserves.

Immediately after signing the treaties, Ottawa began violating their provisions. Chiefs from the different nations began discussing the situation and possible courses of action. Major conferences were organized in the early 1880s as their situation deteriorated. To deal with this, Ottawa made it illegal in 1885 for people to leave their reserves without the signed permission of the Indian agent or another white male. Laws passed in 1884 and 1885 made it illegal to organize politically. In the following decades, land claims mounted as reserves were not properly allocated or were reduced in size. Faced with the prospect of losing such cases, in 1927 Ottawa made it illegal for councils to raise money to hire lawyers. The effect was that First Nations could not use the courts at all. This law severely undermined band governance and remained in effect until 1951. It is difficult to overestimate or even imagine the effect the denial of access to legal advice would have on any government.

One of the strengths of governance in many First Nations was the fact that women often played a major role in leadership and decision-making. Such First Nations were centuries ahead of Europe or the British colonies. The Indian Act terminated the woman's role and deliberately imposed male domination in the councils. Chiefs had been hereditary or elected by consensus and decisions had been made by consensus. The Act gave bands the option of adopting the European municipal systems of elections. There was little or no interest in this, so an amendment of 1880 allowed Ottawa to impose elective councils. Reserves responded by "electing" hereditary chiefs and councillors or maintaining their old government in parallel with the elected ones whose decisions were ignored.

Indian agents were not fooled, and an amendment of 1884 allowed Ottawa to depose chiefs for "dishonesty, intemperance or immorality," that is, for any reason Ottawa identified. In 1920 agents were empowered to ban hereditary rule, in 1935 they were given authority to direct council meetings and cast tie votes. Tie votes had never occurred under the consensus system. The DIA spent decades trying to wipe out the vestiges of the traditional system and the long struggle led to division and a serious weakening of First Nations governance. That was and remains a convenient excuse for maintaining power in the hands of the DIA.

The imposition of elected chiefs and councils on the bands is now one of the major problems behind disputes over land claims and the question of consultations. The elected councils are dependent on Ottawa for the flow of funds necessary to offset the poverty that colonialism has imposed on them. They are not, therefore, in a good position to demand their rights, and having their agreement to, say, a pipeline project, does not necessarily mean that the band has been adequately consulted. Elected councils are responsible for reserve land, but as a result of several Supreme Court decisions, hereditary chiefs have responsibility for "traditional territories" which are often far more extensive than the reserve. "Adequate consultations" therefore require dealing with both elected and hereditary chiefs, something the government and pipeline companies have not done in BC. In 1985 hereditary councils were permitted once more and some bands went back to that tradition system or to a mixed system. Around 200 bands still hold elections. Interestingly, the Canadian Constitution is also a mixed system of a democracy with a hereditary monarchy.

Though not deliberately designed to undermine band governance, one of the most successful of the developments that helped achieve that goal was the batch of policies that reduced First Nations to poverty. These policies are discussed throughout this book, and in terms of governance, the result of poverty was that band councils were staffed by leaders who lacked high school education let alone university degrees, who would not have travelled widely, and who would have little contact with other First Nations leaders.

Poverty crippled the efforts to organize provincial and regional bodies and there are numerous stories of the hardships endured travelling to meetings and demonstrations. Nevertheless, continuous battles with Ottawa over access to land, the pass laws, interference, elections, treaty violations, education, or the imposition of Canadian law led the bands to continue cooperating. In 1918 the League of Indians was organized, the first national organization. War veterans then took the lead in organizing bands in BC and Ontario into the League of Canadian Indians, but it split into provincial groups in the 1930s and 1940s.

In 1944, the North American Indian Brotherhood was organized, a group that had an input into the parliamentary hearings after the Second World War. It evolved into the National Indian Council or NIC in 1961. These efforts were hampered in part by the question of who to include, which was resolved in 1968 when the NIC split into the National Indian Brotherhood (NIB) and the Canadian Métis Society.

The Trudeau government's1969 White Paper spurred First Nations to greater efforts, and in the 1970s, considerable progress was made in organizing more effective provincial and national bodies to lobby for their interests and obtain regular and adequate funding. In 1982, the NIB became the Assembly of First Nations or AFN which has since grown into a fairly effective organization for lobbying the federal government. Its Grand Chief is now invited to meetings of the prime minister and premiers, but the AFN does not legally represent the 634 First

Nations bands and it cannot make binding agreements with the federal government. It is also dependent on federal funding, and several times Ottawa has reduced that funding, a subtle reminder of who pays the piper and a hint not lost on First Nations who question the independence of the AFN from the government that funds it.

Despite strong resistance, over the decades policies designed to weaken band government met with considerable success so that several bands developed serious problems of governance which were then used to justify continued intervention and dominance by Ottawa. This became part of the "vicious circle" argument at the root of so many aspects of the "Indian problem," namely a situation created by government that is so dire that only government can manage it. In this case it is the rational for the argument that First Nations cannot be entrusted with self-government or that Ottawa must determine the limits of any self-government it permits. That policy is itself colonial.

Some of the damage has had serious and lasting effect. Creating male-dominated governments gave men a privileged position, and privilege affected them the same as it affected white males: no one who has power wants to lose it. When pressure mounted to restore status to First Nations women who had lost it through marriage, there was resistance from male Status Indians because the change would increase the number and power of women on the reserves which would in turn threaten their privileged positions.

The government compromised by giving the councils the right to determine membership and, since councils were male dominated, they tended to deny membership to the women who were regaining Indian status. Those women remain the victims of discrimination because of deliberate government policy, reserve governance remains weaker today because of it, the status of women and their descendants has still not been resolved, and First Nations women are not equal to First Nations men.

Overcoming the effects of dividing nations into many bands is proving to be exceedingly difficult. The Mi'kmaq nation, for example, consists of 27 bands who deal with the federal government, five provincial governments, and numerous municipalities. The 13 bands in Nova Scotia formed the Assembly of Nova Scotia Mi'kmaw Chiefs who are working on self-determination through the Made in Nova Scotia Process. They are making progress, but that would be slowed if they joined with the Mi'kmaq from the other four provinces with their different challenges. Federal politicians have always had it right – "divide and conquer" works.

One important First Nations goal was identified as "self-government," one of the most complicated issues facing them and the federal and provincial governments. First Nations had their own governments before contact, and those governments were never legally extinguished. The BNA Act recognized two orders of government in Canada, federal and provincial, but ignored the fact that there was another order of government before settlement, namely that of First Nations, and it had not disappeared.

The Indian Act illegally took self-government from First Nations and federal and provincial government now have to work with band councils to restore some degree of self-government within the framework of the Canadian Constitution. That is essential because the attempt at cultural genocide failed, First Nations culture is not the same as non-Indigenous culture, and the imposition of the latter on every aspect of First Nations life is at the root of many of the problems discussed in this book.

In response to growing pressure and the Calder Court case, Prime Minister Pierre Trudeau offered a form of municipal arrangement in the 1970s. But municipalities are creatures of the provinces, have self-administration not self-government, have a poor reputation amongst First Nations, and any such governments would still be subordinate to Ottawa. Subsequent attempts to implement municipal government on reserves by the Mulroney and Chrétien governments also met very limited success. Ottawa did, however, introduce some flexibility in the way reserve councils were organized and operated. In the 1970s, Ottawa began turning funds over to reserves for various services, but it did not ensure that mechanisms were in place for the proper management of those funds or that the funds were adequate.

Potential problems were flagged in 1966 by the Auditor General, but the advice was ignored. The result was misuse of funds and a discrediting of the ability of reserves to manage money when the fault was in the failure of the DIA to implement the transfer properly. Ottawa has never responded to repeated requests from the Auditor General for a mandate to audit reserve funds. Some might regard this situation as deliberate sabotage by DIA officials.

The problems of transferring power from the DIA back to reserve councils are enormous. A century of the Indian Act, assimilation, residential schools, racism, poverty, and discrimination undermined culture and traditional governance. Most of the 634 reserves are too small to support effective government. Serious underfunding of all aspects of government activity meant that councils face enormous challenges governing their people, so for self-government to succeed, the funding gap has to be ended, previous damage from underfunding overcome, and stable funding put in place. And what the bands would be "self-governing" is programs devised in Ottawa, not by themselves, and that is, by definition, not self-government but colonialism as long as Ottawa is in charge of the programs. The term "self-government" is, in fact, a misnomer as band councils are responsible to Ottawa, not band members, and the bands administer Ottawa's programs, not their own.

The issue of self-government is also intertwined with land settlement in another vicious circle - without good government on the reserves, Ottawa is reluctant to surrender control of land; without control of land, reserves can not address poverty which is a major cause of their weak government. Self-determination is even more difficult. To some it means the recognition of sovereignty. It also means that First Nations decide who is and is not a Status Indian, not the federal government. Ottawa is not likely to recognize parts of Canada as "sovereign" or let First Nations decide who can benefit from treaty rights.

In the 1970s Ottawa began negotiating self-government agreements as part of the settlement of land claims. Such agreements had to be government-to-government, recognize the authority of the First Nations over their own lives, provide jurisdictional clarity, and cover accountability, financial arrangements, and responsibility. They were part of the solution but could only succeed if other problems were also solved and were therefore a stage in solving the "vicious circle" of Canada's "Indian problem." Since it was the DIA that determined if any reserve was ready for self-government and then approved the terms, the process and outcome remained "colonial."

The first was the James Bay Cree Agreement of 1975, called by some the first modern treaty, the first since the numbered treaty series ended in 1921. In 1993, 14 nations in the Council of Yukon Indians made an agreement providing for a degree of self-government. The 1998 Nisga'a agreement in northern BC was significant in several ways besides providing some degree of self-government but only two of BC's 54 reserves were willing to make similar compromises. In 2010, the Sioux Valley Dakota were the first nation on the prairies to sign a self-government agreement with Ottawa, one that had taken 20 years to negotiate. In these agreements federal and provincial laws prevail if there is a conflict and the nations are released from some aspects of the Indian Act.

First Nations have been taking more and more control of services and they rather than Indian agents are now administering programs on reserves even if they do not control those programs and lack the funds to make them fully effective. An important step forward was the First Nations Fiscal Management Act (FMA) of 2006 which gave bands authority to raise funds and set their own priorities for spending them. A recent example occurred in August 2017 when 23 Anishinabek First Nations in Ontario signed a self-government agreement transferring control and funding of education from DIA to their bands.

This process received another boost in August 2019 when Ottawa signed a self-government agreement with all 40 Anishinabek First Nations which represent 65,000 people across the province of Ontario. The agreement allows them to make decisions concerning leadership, citizenship, government operations, and promoting their culture and language, effectively removing them from four provisions of the Indian Act. It took years to negotiate and is to be ratified in February 2020. In effect the Indian Act is being dismantled clause-by-clause and band-by band because it cannot be reformed any other way.

On December 27, 2017, Jane Philpott, Minister of Indigenous Services, announced that the government was working on a new program for funding services on reserves. Accordingly, by April 2019 around 100 reserves which have good records for financial management (in DIA's judgement) would receive ten-year grants to be spent on those services as they themselves determine. They would no longer have to submit the over 130 annual reports to various federal departments but instead would be accountable to their members for the proper administration of the funds. Ottawa would identify the reserves and the amounts; the reserve councils would have to set goals to which they would be accountable. Details were still to be worked out. The fact that Ottawa is in control of the process underlines the difficulty in escaping from the continued colonialism of the Indian Act.

An indication of how little has been achieved, however, came in a speech Prime Minister Trudeau gave in the House of Commons on February 14, 2018. He announced that work would begin on a new framework to identify rights including the right to self-government. The framework was "to build new mechanisms to recognize Indigenous governments," so Indigenous peoples "are in control of their own destiny, making their own decisions..." Minister of Justice Wilson-Raybould added that she wanted Indigenous communities to "control their own lives..."

If true Reconciliation is to occur and if colonialism is to end, governance of First Nations must be turned over to First Nations. If conditions are attached, then power has been retained by the settler government and colonialism has not ended. First Nations proved centuries ago that they could govern themselves as well if not better than Europeans or settlers, and elements of those traditions survived the enormous effort made to stamp them out. How they govern themselves is their business just as how non-Indigenous Canadians govern themselves is their business.

Canadians are enormously proud that they are no longer governed from London; they do not see the contradiction that First Nations are still governed from Ottawa in violation of the treaties. The solution requires abandoning the idea that bands are being "given" money so Ottawa must control it: Ottawa's money comes from the territory taken from First Nations and they are owed rent on it, just as the treaties say. When non-Indigenous Canadians accept that and implement it, a huge obstacle to Canada's progress and reputation as a nation will have been removed, and progress on every other Indigenous problem will be accelerated.

Chapter 9

Residential Schools and Cultural Genocide

The Executive Summary of the Report of the Truth and Reconciliation Commission (TRC) of 2015 should be compulsory reading for anyone dealing with Indigenous peoples at any level of government, in any major economic or social relationship, in anything to do with Indigenous peoples such as the teaching of history, managing museums, volunteer agencies, or the management of companies working on or near reserves. The report is a superb document that explains the present terrible situation of which no one can be proud, the background and the role of residential schools in that dismal past, much of the context such as colonialism and the Indian Act, and the way forward that all Canadians must struggle towards.

It should be noted that the TRC is a study of the victims of the schools, not of the oppressors and their superiors; it looked at part of the truth, not the "whole truth." It did not, in fact, have authority to examine the perpetrators or assign blame and was scrupulous in sticking to its narrowly defined mandate. Much of this chapter is drawn directly from that report.

In the sixteenth century, Europeans began coming to the Americas for a number of reasons: to make money, to advance their careers, for adventure, to make their kings and countries more powerful, and to "civilize" the inhabitants whom they regarded as "savages," as inferior in almost every way - religion, culture, technology, political organization, even clothing and diet. Apart from scientific matters such as writing and technology, European attitudes reflected a superiority complex that had little basis in fact and in some aspects of governance, relations with the environment, clothing and diet, First Nations societies were superior to those of Europe. First Nations societies were simply "different," so when Europeans could demonstrate superior elements such as weapons, First Nations were quick to adopt them, and when they could not, such as with diet and clothing, they did not. That bothered Europeans who assumed that everything they did or believed was superior, and it was best for others to adopt their ways as quickly as possible.

Convinced of their superiority, Europeans set out to Christianize and "civilize" the people they mistakenly viewed as "heathen" or "savages." An important part of the French colonial effort was the dispatch of missionaries to First Nations villages to bring the word of God and change the way people lived. First Nations were interested in different interpretations of creation and life and death, less so in changing their moral values and the way they lived. Gradually they were converted to Christianity but that tended to be a superficial addition to a strong retention of belief in their own religious teachings and values.

The work of missionaries in First Nations villages was not completely successful, so the Church established a few schools in which children would be taken out of their villages and exposed continuously to French and Christian culture. Few children attended and they did not become "brown French Canadians." In 1834, the British established the first residential school in Upper Canada and there were several of them by the 1850s. They were modelled on reform schools which were designed to deal with problem children, not on private ones which usually catered to elites, and they often had low expectations of their students, an attitude which is often self-fulfilling. In these schools First Nations children could presumably be educated and learn the trades that would allow them to integrate successfully into the colonial economy. Though the schools were not successful, the model was retained.

In the middle decades of the nineteenth century a profound change occurred in the relations of First Nations with white settlers and their colonial governments. From being valued allies in warfare and essential partners in the fur trade, First Nations became obstacles to continued settlement which was a top priority of the colonial governments. White settlers and their governments decided that First Nations had to be assimilated and integrated into Canadian society, fully Christianized and civilized, and that their culture, values, language, and governance had to be stamped out. By becoming Canadians, they would "disappear," an essential element of the deliberate policy of colonialism. The only ethnic groups forced to go to specific schools because of their race were Indigenous peoples, and that is racism.

The main instrument chosen for this transformation was the expansion of the existing, failed system of residential schools. The citizens of the United Province of Canada and their government had wonderful and expensive ambitions and dreams, like building canals along the St. Lawrence and Great Lakes and railways to the Atlantic and the Pacific. Ottawa had little money for educating First Nations but that was not a priority for another reason. Since contact in 1600, the population of First Nations in what would become Canada had probably declined from around 500,000 to under 200,000 and was still declining rapidly due to disease. Educating them would be a small and shrinking problem.

At the same time, volunteers were readily available for the task, namely the Catholic and Protestant churches. Missionary activity was a well-established role of these religions, supported by congregations eager to expand their flocks and spread the word of God. The churches had been involved in missionary work and teaching for centuries and had run residential schools in Canada. Partnering with the colonial governments to "civilize" First Nations was a welcome duty and challenge. The partnership of the federal government and the churches was perfect for both sides and the fact that residential schools had failed in the past was ignored.

For the Catholics, the schools would be operated by priests and nuns who received no salaries; for the Protestants, by teachers whose religious zeal would help overcome low salaries and poor conditions. For Ottawa, there were even more financial advantages to farming out its responsibilities. It was decided that the schools would be largely self-supporting. Children would attend classes for half the day, work for the other half producing farm products for consumption and sale, making furniture and clothing, cutting wood, gardening, operating the kitchen and laundry, and maintaining the buildings. This could be defended as useful training for the real world. It was, in fact, forced child labour and racial discrimination - no students in non-Indigenous schools were expected to do any work to support the schools.

As if this were not enough, the government cut subsidies in the 1890s which produced a health crisis. That led to a scathing report in 1907 on health conditions and the lack of equipment, training, and facilities. It was written by the government's Chief Medical Health Officer, Dr. Peter Bryce, who was punished for continuing to criticize the government when his report was ignored. Costs were cut again during the Depression which almost led to the collapse of the whole system. Per student federal spending on the schools was always considerably lower than that of the provinces even though half the students' time was spent supporting the schools financially. In 1937, Manitoba spent three times as much per student at its School for the Deaf and in 1966, Ottawa was spending $694-$1,193 per student compared to Saskatchewan which was spending $3,300-$9,855. The residential schools were designed to cost Ottawa little, one of the few objectives that was achieved.

The federal government never established an overall plan for the schools. They were run by the Catholic orders, the Anglicans, Methodists, Presbyterians, and the United Church. There was no common goals or curricula. They were not coordinated with provincial education systems or with the needs and opportunities the students would face in the future. There was no system of inspection and the inspection reports that were produced were not systematically acted on and were usually ignored. Principals and teachers asked for instructions, few were provided. In 1955, the federal regulation for the schools was four pages long compared to the 91 pages of the Manitoba Education Act. One of the worst failings was that children were denied the experience of seeing adults raising children, and graduates of the schools had problems as parents, as did their own children. The effects of that are still present.

One expense the government had to make was building the schools, and in this the goal of saving money clearly outweighed both the need for a satisfactory environment for learning and the actual health and safety of the students. Often the schools were not located on appropriate sites in terms of drainage. They were poorly designed, poorly constructed, poorly ventilated, and poorly heated. They lacked proper health facilities and in one case the infirmary was located above the smelly lavatory. In these conditions, students succumbed to tuberculosis by the thousand. Machinery was not properly protected, and accidents were frequent, including deaths. These were blamed on the students. Non-indigenous Canadians remain proud of the investments in their educational facilities in the same period – state of the art technology, beautiful architecture, trees and playgrounds.

Staff were inadequately qualified for their jobs. Principals were selected according to their positions in the churches, not as educators, and staff were poorly supervised. Religious zeal was the main qualification for teachers, many of whom were not qualified to teach. As late as 1955, a quarter of those hired by the DIA lacked teachers' certificates. Because they were residential schools, teachers were responsible for all aspects of the students' life, issues like welfare and guidance, for which they were unqualified. Poor salaries resulted in high turnover so there was a lack of experience and continuity. These conditions produced problems with the students, and the inevitable result was excessive discipline.

Conditions in the schools were abominable. They were often over-crowded. Rooms were cold and drafty. Students were often hungry. Food was so poorly prepared it made students throw up and some of them were forced to eat that food again. The milk supply was inadequate because cows were sick due to a lack of funding for adequate barns. Food did not meet federal nutritional guidelines. A report of 1940 said that the system failed to meet minimum standards. It was ignored.

The DIA had no policy on discipline, so each school was essentially free to act as teachers and officials wished. Discipline was therefore harsh, including strapping on the bare back, humiliation, a diet of bread-and-water, prison rooms, students chained together or to beds, students kicked, punched, and thrown against walls and hit with sticks or forced to sit in snow without proper clothing. Officials dominated personal lives to the point that marriages were arranged for older students and students were prevented from marrying people who had not attended a residential school.

Fire was a danger due to poor conditions and sabotage with at least 37 attempts to burn the schools. Fifty schools did burn down, 170 more experienced fires, and there were at least 40 deaths partly because fire escapes were locked in order to prevent students from running away. At least 33 died running away, some because there was no effective policy until 1973 for schools to notify police of missing children. Some of those caught were charged with stealing their clothes. There are no reliable estimates of deaths because records were not properly kept, hundreds of thousands of files were destroyed, and government and churches have fought tenaciously to keep files secret. They still do. The deaths included infanticide and abortions. The TRC concluded that at least 5,200 children died and that until the 1950s the death rate was roughly five times higher than that for non-Indigenous children. Almost half of recorded deaths were from tuberculosis, most of the others indicated no cause.

The goals of teaching Christianity, civilization, basic schooling, and trades were subverted from the beginning by the weaknesses and contradictions in the system. Since the schools were to be self-sufficient to the largest degree possible, a top priority was placed on producing farm products. The concept of a 50-50 split between classroom and "apprenticeship" broke down as students found themselves doing more and more physical work in the barns, fields, gardens and kitchens. With government subsidies inadequate, schools sold cream and butter, feeding the students with skim milk which contributed to a daily caloric intake well below what was needed, which would affect their ability to study, work or remain healthy.

Study became simple memorization; work was the routine chopping of firewood; farm skills were easily learned and then repeated. It often took three years to acquire one grade of schooling. As late as 1960 the failure rate in Grade 1 was over 40% and only half the grade 2 students made it to grade 6. It was a system made in hell which did not produce the concept of Christianity envisaged by the religious congregations that supported the schools. Somehow the churches were able to keep conditions secret from the congregations that supported them.

The real expansion of the system began in the 1880s after the treaties were signed and First Nations moved to their reserves. By 1930, there were 80 schools across Canada, and the maximum number was 139. Overall 150,000 students passed through these schools, with enrollment peaking in 1956 at 11,500. But throughout this period, half of First Nations children remained on the reserves, possibly attending day schools.

At first attendance at residential schools was not compulsory. However, since the government was not providing schools on many reserves as required by the treaties, parents who were eager to have their children obtain the same education as whites sent them to the schools. When they heard of the conditions from their children, many were reluctant to send them back. Parents who did not send their children to the schools were fined, imprisoned, and denied food, and officials entered homes and physically removed children over the objections of parents.

Despite these efforts, attendance remained low. In 1894, attendance was made compulsory though there was no legal authority for such a policy, and the RCMP began, in effect, kidnapping children. By then running away was a well-established pattern so children were often sent to schools hundreds of miles from their homes. Some escapees walked hundreds of miles to their homes, dozens died in the effort. Some of them would have survived only school officials did not notify the police of their absence in time for them to launch effective searches. The tragic death of Chanie Wenjack in 1966 was turned into an award-winning album and novel by Gord Downie in 2016. It became a valued teaching tool, an indication of the growing awareness of the residential schools and the need for Reconciliation. The law on compulsory attendance remained in the Indian Act until 2014, 18 years after the last school closed!

Amongst the worst features of the residential schools was the systematic abuse of the students. There was abuse of every kind - verbal, mental, physical, and sexual. It started on the day of arrival with the deliberate policy of breaking the students' faith in their own culture, with "putting them down." Their braids were shaved off, their beautiful beaded moccasins and jackets thrown in the garbage. Speaking their own languages was punished by the forced eating of soap, physical abuse, and putting needles through their tongues. They were humiliated daily.

A favourite punishment was tugging on the ears, to the point of permanent damage to hearing. Other punishments caused permanent damage to limbs and organs. Children who wet their beds were paraded before the classes in their wet clothes. They were told they were "savages." Students were also subjected to scientific experiments, the sort of thing one normally associates with Nazi Germany. One experiment involved reducing meals to evaluate the effects on health. They were discouraged from going home during the summer and parents were discouraged from visiting and told to speak English during visits.

At night the abuse degenerated into sexual attacks. The first known case of sexual abuse occurred in 1886. Nothing was done. Five years later new allegations against the same person were made and he was allowed to resign. Students would be ordered to go to a room, would be molested, and would be warned of serious consequences if they complained including eternal damnation. Some students were abused on a weekly basis for years – thousands of cases of rape. All forms of abuse were perpetrated, by both sexes on both sexes. Incidents were kept secret from the police, superior authorities, and families. Investigations were thwarted. Convicted offenders were retained on staff or transferred to other schools. Records were not kept.

One of the worst aspects of the abuse was that as students matured in the system, they began using abuse to force younger students to steal food for them and to provide sexual favours. That, rather than Christian love and charity, was the education they would take back to their villages and families. In order to survive, they also learned to lie and play favourites. That remains the base of much suffering today because the effects last for generations and help explain why the victims kept silent for decades. It is a cause of the ongoing tragedy of "Missing and Murdered Indigenous Women and Girls."

The system almost collapsed in 1945 after 15 years of financial restraints, and it was well known throughout the system that it was a failure. The use of day schools increased, and in 1951 students were permitted to go to provincial schools. By 1960, there were more First Nations students in provincial schools than in residential ones, but this was another system of assimilation, and a more effective one. First Nations continued to demand schools on reserves and under their own control, but Ottawa resisted. From the 1940s, the schools were increasingly used as orphanages and within two decades, half the students were essentially there as child-welfare cases. The schools were not capable of dealing with those additional problems, but some children spent their entire childhood in these schools. In 1968, Ottawa took direct control from the churches and began closing the schools, the number dropping from 60 to 45 in 1970, the last one closing in 1996. But they did not change in those last 40 years.

The effect of these horrors was to leave the students traumatized, guilt-ridden, and facing serious challenges living in either Indigenous or non-Indigenous society. The survivors often had and still have problems coping with life, jobs, family, sex, marriage, and parenting. This led to a high rate of suicide, to self-destructive behaviour, to alcohol and drug abuse, to the perpetuation of abuse on others, the acceptance of crime, the distrust of officials and authority, the formation of gangs for protection and identity, and violence as a way of life. The negative effects lasted for generations - the grandchildren of residential school survivors suffer these problems to a greater degree than others. To some degree the schools were successful in the short term in destroying language and culture as some students could not communicate with their families when they returned home and would not teach their children their customs.

The combination of shame and effective cover up of these crimes meant that little was known of this human tragedy until stories began to emerge in the 1980s. What young teenager would tell his/her parents that they had become victimized, had had abortions, had become abusers themselves, had watched babies being killed? But more and more survivors started to come forward, and authorities in both church and civil society realized that there was a crisis in the residential school system. The numbers seemed incredible, but they were correct - thousands and thousands of cases of sexual abuse, almost all of them covered up by authorities in the schools and amongst those administering the schools and responsible for them.

It also became clear to more and more Canadians that the schools violated several categories of the United Nations Convention on the Prevention of Genocide. Eventually the churches began to apologize, the United Church in 1986, the Catholic Oblate Order in 1991, the Anglican Church in 1993, and the Presbyterian Church in 1994. In 2006 the Catholic Church, which ran 72% of the schools, agreed to pay $25M in compensation but only paid $3.7M. Pope Francis refused to apologize and would not meet victims at a February 2019 Vatican summit on sexual abuse. On July 13, 2019, the Anglican Church apologized for the spiritual harm inflicted by their residential schools. Their 1993 apology covered physical, emotional and sexual abuse and the 2019 apology reflects the Truth and Reconciliation Report's Call for Action #60 which recommends that churches accept Indigenous spirituality.

People began launching lawsuits against individuals, churches and the government - by 2001 there were 8,500, by 2005 over 18,000. These were combined into the largest class-action lawsuit in Canadian history. One year later Ottawa accepted the Indian Residential Schools Settlement Agreement. In total, the claims of 78,000 students were recognized, a figure that does not include the thousands of students who had died and those from some schools which were not included such as the ones in Newfoundland and Labrador which were not part of Canada until 1949. The abuse was not the exception; it had been normal, rampant and systemic.

Of the claims, 30,939 cases were resolved. Claimants could receive $10,000 for the first year in school, $3,000 for additional years for a total cost to Ottawa of $2,690,000,000. The settlement also provided funding for dealing with abuse, health problems, and for creating means to address the legacy as well as establishing the Truth and Reconciliation Commission (TRC). Prime Minister Stephen Harper and other political leaders apologized in 2008, though it was not clear that the government acknowledged that the schools represented cultural genocide. As with previous acknowledgements of wrongdoing, this apology suggested that the wrongs were in the past and did not address the fact that the federal government was still pursuing many policies that were inherently colonial and constituted continued cultural genocide

The extent of the disaster was not revealed until the TRC published its final report in 2015. As of September 2013, $1.6B had been paid for 105,000 cases. On November 24, 2017, PM Justin Trudeau apologized for crimes committed in the schools in Newfoundland and Labrador. One year earlier 1,000 of those survivors had won a lawsuit for $50M. Newfoundland and Labrador Premier Dwight Ball promised at the time to make an apology but as of July 2019 the arrangements for that had not yet been finalized.

The settlements have not gone entirely smoothly. From the beginning both the federal government and the churches have used various arguments and spent large amounts of money fighting to keep documents secret, documents that survivors need to support their claims. In one such case involving the notorious St. Anne's Residential School which employed an electric chair to discipline students, the Department of Justice spent $2.3M in legal fees fighting to keep documents secret. The school was open from 1902 to 1976, but that court battle occurred from 2013 to 2018, well into the regime of the current government, long after the Ontario Superior Court ordered Ottawa to turn the documents over in 2014 and after the 2015 Report of the TRC. Indeed, the Report of the TRC is based on a fraction of the written evidence (though how large or small a fraction will never be known), and the written evidence is the tip of the iceberg since neither perpetrator nor victim would have recorded many/most sexual assaults.

The inability to obtain documents has limited payments (and saved the government money) because victims have not been able to prove the degree of damage they suffered. The battles over documents have also added to their trauma and legal costs so the residential school system continues to inflict suffering on its survivors. And the number of survivors declines as the older ones die off, without compensation, without closure. Time has always been on the government's side and it has used it effectively. The latest small victory by a survivor was won in mid-April 2019. As of May, 2019 99% of claims had been completed and 89% had been settled at a cost of $3.2B.

One outcome of the T&R inquiry was the establishment of the National Centre for Truth and Reconciliation in Winnipeg under Director Ry Moran. It is the repository for the documents collected during the inquiry, but it also has a watching brief on how the settlement and recommendations are being implemented. In late 2018, Moran visited seven locations across Canada to meet survivors and discuss their experiences with the settlement and the follow-up to the TRC. These meetings and other ways of collecting feedback will lead to a report to inform Canadians of progress and reaction and perhaps to changes to the healing process and other outcomes of the Commission.

Three of the Calls for Action by the TRC concerned work to preserve Indigenous languages, that is, to reverse the considerable degree of success the residential schools and other policies of assimilation had achieved in destroying that crucial aspect of Indigenous culture. The degree of "cultural genocide" in terms of language can be measured – today 75% of Canada's existing Indigenous languages are endangered.

On February 6, 2019, Ottawa tabled legislation to establish the Office of the Commissioner of Indigenous Languages to protect and promote the languages and Bill C-91 was passed in June. While welcomed as a step in the right direction, it remains to be seen when it will be established, what power and budget it will have, and what it will achieve. In a sense, Ottawa is catching up because considerable progress is being made throughout education systems and elsewhere in the recognition, teaching, presentation, and promotion of these languages.

The CBC Indigenous Unit established a website called *Beyond 94* to monitor progress on the implementation of the TRC's 94 Calls to Action. Its July 8, 2019 update lists 10 under "Completed," including appointing an Inquiry into Missing and Murdered Indigenous Women and Girls and several minor achievements such as restoring funding for TV programs. It lists 27 under "Not Started," including publishing annual reports on the number of children in care, publishing annual reports on funding for education and outcomes, and repudiating the doctrines of Discovery and terra nullius. It lists 23 under "Projects Proposed," including closing gaps in health between Indigenous and non-Indigenous Canadians, closing the gap in incarceration rates, and eliminating the discrepancy between federal spending on students on and off reserve. It lists 23 as "Underway," including implementing Jordan's Principle. Many of the Calls for Action could have been done, many require actions by non-governmental bodies, many are costly and will take years. But an examination of *Beyond 94* may help explain a poll commissioned by the CBC (June 10) that indicated that two-thirds of First Nations do not believe the federal government respects their community and identities.

Starting in the 1920s, over 200,000 Indigenous children were sent to over 700 day-schools across Canada, more students than went to residential schools. In these schools they also endured the same sorts of abuses as those in the residential schools, but not at night or on weekends. A movement began to seek redress in the 1980s, and a court action was launched in 2006 seeking $15B in compensation. Approximately 120-140,000 of those students are still alive. On December 6, 2018, Ottawa settled the class action suit in principle. The settlement provides $200M for healing, wellness, languages and legal fees. The details were agreed on March 12, 2019 and approved by a Federal Court in August. It provides compensation ranging from $10,000 to $200,000 depending on the degree of suffering. Various criticisms were made, and court actions launched while the survivors die off at the rate of 2,000 a year. Those included in the class-action lawsuit can begin filing claims, a process that will extend over 30 months.

The residential and day school disasters were not isolated incidents in Canada's past. Canadians cannot just apologize, pay compensation, implement the recommendations of the Truth and Reconciliation Commission (which will take many years), rename a few buildings, hide a few statues and move on mumbling "what's past is past." The schools were part of a colonial system that included the reserves, the theft of lands and much more that has not been corrected or, in some cases, even admitted.

In June 2018, on the tenth anniversary of PM Stephen Harper's apology, an Angus Reid poll showed that 53% of Canadians felt Canada "spends too much time apologizing for residential schools." In fact, there have been two apologies – PM Harper's in 2008 for the schools in the nine provinces and PM Trudeau's in 2017 for those in Newfoundland which had been separate from Canada before 1949. The argument of "too many apologies" is itself a denial of past mistakes – apologizing for one wrong cannot absolve government from apologizing for a different one.

There is also a paradox in Canadian history that must be acknowledged. The federal government is extremely jealous of its own responsibilities and has spent 150 years trying to expand into areas of provincial jurisdiction such as education. At the same time, it failed to meet its exclusive treaty, constitutional, governmental and moral responsibilities for the education of First Nations children. This paradoxical policy continues today. In the residential schools it offloaded the responsibility and the cost on the churches, the students, and then the provinces. It has even tried to interpret the Constitution as saying it is only responsible for First Nations who live on reserves.

Canadians must try to understand why their government deliberately and knowingly managed the residential school system for 100 years in a way that can only be termed racial discrimination. It was guilty of cultural genocide as the Truth and Reconciliation Commission said after thoroughly documenting the evidence. Attitudes are shifting in the right direction, but Canadians and their governments have a long way to go towards Reconciliation.

Chapter 10

Incarceration Rates: From Zero to Infinity

In 2019, the incarceration rates for Indigenous Canadians are eight times as high as those of non-Indigenous Canadians. But when Cartier arrived in the Gulf of St. Lawrence in 1534 there were no First Nations in jail. The incarceration rate was zero and had probably always been zero. Like Europeans, First Nation could rob, rape and murder members of other nations, but unlike Europeans, it was rare for them to rob, rape and murder members of their own nation. There were exceptions, and crimes were dealt with by execution, banishment, and shaming, but there were no jails in the villages that Europeans encountered as they made their way across North America. Obviously, something went terribly wrong between 1534 and 2019.

The Europe of 1600 faced a severe crime problem as it had for centuries and would continue to face long into the future. It was a society based on exploitation, with kings and nobles living as extravagantly as possibly at the expense of a peasant class that paid crushing rates of taxation. There were continuous revolts against nobles, kings and foreign domination, and crime was commonplace as the poor stole or hunted illegally in order to survive. Such a society required a substantial apparatus of laws, police, courts, informants, jails, torture, and public executions. That system was brought to North America including the continent's first jails. First Nations invariably ran afoul of the white man's laws, but the numbers imprisoned were limited as their population was rapidly declining and was being pushed to the margins of settled land.

The Northwest Rebellion resulted in the trial of 44 First Nations people. The standards were lower than those for white and Métis rebels, and led to one of the worst miscarriages of justice in Canadian history. The revolt of the Métis and some white settlers was fully justified, but the grievances of the First Nations were far more serious. With a few individual exceptions, they did not join because leaders such as Chiefs Poundmaker and Big Bear ensured that they did not. Doing so required great courage, perseverance, and political skill. They should have been thanked or left alone, but they and several others were arrested and imprisoned and six were hanged. The Rebellion was deliberately and wrongly used to break opposition to the "civilizing" policies of the 1876 Indian Act. On May 23, 2019, Prime Minister Justin Trudeau exonerated Poundmaker of treason, part of the government's continued efforts at Reconciliation.

The systematic criminalization of Canada's First Nations began with the imposition of the numbered treaties. The First Nations retained the right to hunt and fish on the 95% of the land they surrendered unless it was utilized for agriculture or other purposes. White settlers also wanted to hunt, and the combined pressure of First Nations and white hunters depleted stocks of fish and game. To manage wildlife, the federal and provincial governments established conservation rules. These laws were necessary, but in the case of the First Nations, they represented an illegal, massive, and unilateral violation of the treaties and a threat to their survival. Naturally they continued to hunt and fish. In BC, types of fishing gear used for centuries were declared illegal along with fishing sites and whole stretches of rivers. On the agricultural front, some First Nations had successfully adopted farming and were competing with white farmers on local markets, so governments forbade them selling without a licence.

Throughout history peoples of all races and colours have reacted to such situations in the same way - they break the law. In terms of hunting and fishing, First Nations would have a higher incidence of "crime" than whites because hunting was a major part of their economy and food supply. Turning them into lawbreakers bred a negative view of the police, courts, justice system, and law. Another negative effect of these laws and of sports hunting by whites was that the protein content of the Indigenous diet deteriorated steadily with inevitable consequences in terms of weakened resistance to disease.

As the government systematically violated the treaties, First Nations leaders worked together to deal with the problems they were facing. The government had deliberately split nations such as the Blackfoot or Cree into many small reserves distant from each other, a typical policy of "divide and conquer." In order to discuss the problems of dealing with Ottawa and plan common strategies, chiefs and others travelled from reserve to reserve. To stop that, Ottawa adopted a regulation in 1885 saying they needed the written permission of an agent or other white settler to leave a reserve. That was a violation of law, of human rights, and, most importantly, of the treaties, a regulation like those used to control American slaves before 1864. Naturally they violated it.

First Nations knew the laws were stacked against them and that they were ill-equipped to defend their causes, so they hired lawyers. In 1927, Ottawa made it illegal for them to raise money to hire lawyers, effectively ending their access to the courts. This law was enforced until 1951 and helps explain why so little progress was made in winning legal and other battles before the 1970s.

As part of the "civilizing" policy, missionaries demanded that the government outlaw traditions that might hinder the complete acceptance of Christianity. One of the most important was the Potlach in BC in which people accumulated desired objects for years and then hosted a huge celebration to give away their wealth to prove their worth and status. This was outlawed in 1889 even though Christians have similar though less extravagant practices and European kings reinforced their power by giving huge estates to their supporters. People then had less incentive to work to acquire gifts to distribute but they continued to hold smaller Potlaches in secret so for decades the laws were systematically tightened without destroying the practice. On the prairies the Sun Dance was viewed as pagan by missionaries and Ottawa duly outlawed it and other dances in 1885.

Another cause of criminalization was the outlawing of drinking on reserves. These laws were introduced at different times across the country and gradually applied off reserves. The causes were many, and some bands asked the government to ban alcohol from reserves. But the effect was the same as when Prohibition was applied to other Canadians in the 1920s. The ban had some positive effects, but it did not stop a considerable number of people from drinking and running afoul of the police. The law also prevented them from working in establishments where alcohol was present such as hotels, restaurants, and drug stores. In 1876, they were forbidden to enter pool halls, the assumption being that playing pool kept them from working which it somehow did not do to whites.

By 1900, First Nations could be incarcerated for hunting, fishing, dancing, singing, drinking, giving gifts, being on much of Canada's territory without permission, being in a pool room, participating in shows, stampedes, or exhibitions or wearing traditional costumes without permission. That is after they survived the residential schools where they learned the advantages of bullying and physical and sexual abuse, which could also lead to incarceration.

Many were imprisoned and are in prison today because they cannot pay a fine and the reason for that is the poverty that resulted from government policies. The choice of fine or jail time automatically ensured that poor people such as First Nations had far higher rates of incarceration than richer people. Jail then exposed them to violence, hardened criminals, mistreatment, and isolation, conditions that resulted in mental conditions and in them joining gangs in order to survive. They emerged hardened rather than reformed, and far more likely to become repeat offenders than those who could pay fines. This situation has been documented for decades in study after study and governments have done little about it including the current ones.

Catholic and Protestant churches pressured governments to apply similar morality laws to non-Indigenous Canadians but were largely unsuccessful except in the case of Prohibition. The churches succeeded in having governments apply them to First Nations partly because the government had dictatorial control over them through the law, the police, the justice system, the reserve system, and the Indian agents, and faced no political backlash from voters because they could not vote until 1961.

By 1951, the Canadian government had realized that some aspects of its own treatment of First Nations violated the standards of human rights it was promoting at the United Nations. The infamous pass system was abolished, and it became legal to hire lawyers. It was discovered that First Nations could "hold their liquor" as well as others could and that the idea that they could not was like the false science that suggested whites were more intelligent than people of colour.

That should have led to a decline in the incarceration rate which was around 2% of all prisoners before 1960. Instead, the number and percentage has been rising steadily since the 1950s and the trend appears to have accelerated in the last decade. That applies to First Nations, Métis, and Inuit and to all categories of inmates - young, old, female, male, especially young female. In 2017, 5% of Canadian adults were Indigenous but they constituted 28% of the nation's male inmates and 43% of female inmates. In 2017, 8% of Canada's youth were Indigenous but they make up 46% of prison populations, up from 21% a decade earlier.

In Saskatchewan, the proportion of youth in prison who were Indigenous rose from 70% in 2007 to 92% in 2017. In Manitoba, over 80% of the youth in prisons are Indigenous. In BC, the proportion of the young Indigenous females in jail jumped from 32% to 60% in the last decade though they accounted for only 5% of the province's young population. Overall the number of youth in prison has been decreasing but for Indigenous youth it has been exploding. In Quebec, over half the complaints of police misconduct brought before the Bureau of Independent Investigations since 2016 were by Indigenous people who constitute around 2% of the population. These statistics are not even complete - Alberta has not released the relevant figures since 2012.

Two of the most serious aspects of this situation are that high incarceration rates not only perpetuate the policy of assimilation, but they assimilate First Nations into the worst aspects of non-Indigenous society, association with criminals and the criminal justice system. There are numerous reasons for this trend. The main one is poverty and the main cause of that is the policies adopted and maintained by the federal government over the past 150 years, policies documented throughout this book.

The Harper government's mandatory minimum sentencing legislation removed the capacity of the courts to impose lesser punishment to reflect extenuating circumstances. That legislation fell heaviest on Indigenous people and was not rescinded by the current government. But the main problem is probably racism, and while it is difficult to prove racism, it is also difficult to convince people that racism is not present when a justice system overwhelmingly dominated by white people systematically treats coloured people far harsher than white ones.

Trial by peers was the principle of justice adopted in the famous Magna Carta of 1215; in Canada both whites and First Nations are tried by white Canadians. That was the case in the wrongful conviction of the Mi'kmaq Donald Marshall for murder in 1971 – he was acquitted in 1983 and exonerated in 1990. The RCAP Commission of 1996 criticized the racial bias of juries and the 1999 Manitoba Aboriginal Justice Commission recommended that lawyers not be allowed to dismiss potential jurors without cause, a system that allows potential First Nations jurors to be eliminated from juries.

The recent Boushie case in Saskatchewan underlined that fact: in the trial of a white farmer, Gerald Stanley, for killing a First Nations youth, Colten Boushie on August 9, 2016, all the potential Indigenous people were eliminated from the jury. The Minister of Justice, Jody Wilson-Raybould, said "we can and must do better," but nothing was done. Finally, governments have been able to ignore the "Indian problem" they created and maintained by failing to teach anything remotely resembling objective, factual Canadian history for the past 150 years. In one of its first acts, the Ontario Conservative government elected in 2018 reversed a decision to include serious and accurate Indigenous history in the school curriculum.

Once in jail it is more difficult for Indigenous people to get out than for others. They are more likely to be denied parole, to have to serve the maximum sentence, or to be put in solitary confinement. The latter creates another "vicious circle," namely mental problems and violence which perpetuates the length of time in jail. It also prevents them from attending cultural programs or healing lodges. If they come from remote communities, they are less likely to have the benefit of family visits. They are more likely to be released without the benefit of the gradual adjustment provided by day-parole.

Once released they are more likely to be sent back for violating parole or probation conditions because of distance, the expense of travel, or mental illness. Over half of Indigenous inmates may in fact be in prison not to serve the original sentence but as a result of the administrative decisions of non-Indigenous officials who have the power to decide how long any inmate must remain in jail and under what circumstances.

All this reinforces a vicious circle - First Nations know they are discriminated against, resent it, react to it, display an "attitude problem," and the predominantly white police and judicial system react to that with carding, harsher treatment and denial of bail and parole. It is also clear that there is widespread ignorance throughout the justice system of Indigenous history, culture, conditions, and matters like the treaties. Persons with criminal records cannot serve on juries, so the high incidence of crime reduces the pool of First Nations eligible for jury duty, another element in the vicious circle. One small improvement was a 2018 Supreme Court decision that a test used to help determine eligibility for parole was biased against Indigenous people, a case brought by a Métis prisoner, Jeffrey Ewert.

Another factor is carding and racial profiling. Carding is the police practice of stopping citizens for no reason to determine if there was a reason, such as liquor or marijuana on the breath, problems with the driving licence or car registration, or too many people in the car. There is a valid reason for carding, namely saving lives. If the police stop 10,000 people at random, they are bound to find that some of them are violating some traffic law, so punishing them will make Canadians safer. But carding is acceptable only if it is done fairly and applied equally to all citizens regardless of age, sex, colour, ethnicity, or place of residence. That is patently not the case, because the police have been found repeatedly applying carding disproportionately to Indigenous and other coloured Canadians.

In Vancouver, Indigenous people make up 2-3% of the population, but 16% of the people the police stopped for no apparent reason between 2008 and 2017 were Indigenous. Like all drivers, some of them were probably guilty of some traffic violation. Stopping six times as many people from any group will produce a disproportionate number of "crimes" for that group, and carding is one of the reasons for the high incarceration rate for First Nations.

It will remain so as long as it is practiced and there is little evidence Canadian governments are prepared to stop the practice. Indeed, the current government has gone in the opposite direction as the new law dealing with the possible effects of legalizing marijuana, Bill C-45, gives the police more power over individuals stopped at checkpoints. It is noteworthy that police forces that have the time and resources to engage in carding do not apparently have adequate time and resources to deal with missing and murdered Indigenous people.

The problem of racism amongst police forces was highlighted in December 2018, by three reports. The reputation for racism of the Thunder Bay police was confirmed by the December 12 report of Gerry McNeilly, Ontario's independent police review director. It was described as a "scathing" indictment of police failure to investigate the murders of

Indigenous men, and McNeilly ordered a re-investigation of nine cases. Two days later, Senator Murray Sinclair released a report on the board that oversees the Thunder Bay police. He said it had failed and recommended it be suspended for a year, which was done immediately.

The Board was reconstituted but in May 2019, the Ontario government removed a member, John Cyr, when it was discovered that he had written a letter supporting the controversial views on Indigenous people of Senator Lynn Beyak. Indigenous leaders also want Mayor Bill Mauro removed from the Board. One of them, Alvin Fiddler, said it would be difficult to fight racism if the city's leadership was not fully supportive, a likely reference to foot-dragging in providing the police the resources recommended in the December report.

Thunder Bay has the highest rate of hate crime in Canada, a situation thoroughly documented in the excellent book *Seven Fallen Feathers* by Tanya Talaga. In June 2019 the inquiry into the nine deaths was announced. It will be done by a body including First Nations, external investigators, experts and the police excluding any police involved in the original investigations. The composition of the committee was announced on August 2, and the 22 members represent a broad spectrum of views, interests, and expertise. They expect to report within a year.

On December 10, the Ontario Human Rights Commission released a damning report on racism in the Toronto Police based on a study of data from 2010 to 2017. These reports recommended training, not punishment of those guilty, and there are questions as to how effective training has been. There is some evidence of progress concerning racism in the police forces, but Canada has a great distance to go before racism is eliminated in the police forces and it will take years after that before First Nations accept that it has finally ended and the wounds healed.

Sadly, some First Nations who might have committed a crime never made it to court because they were killed by the police during the arrest process. Criminals sometimes resist arrest and police carry firearms to ensure they can enforce the law, so it is not surprising that in Canada some citizens are shot and killed during encounters with police. What is shocking is the number and ratio of Indigenous people amongst those killed. Since 2000, police in Manitoba have killed 19 people in the course of carrying out their duties - 11 of them or 60% were Indigenous.

In the same period, 16 people were killed by police in Saskatchewan, 10 of them Indigenous. On June 19, 2017, Austin Eaglechief died in a high-speed police chase in Saskatoon. He had stolen a truck and rammed a police cruiser. For two years all the information available came from police sources, including an explanation of why two shots were fired at the truck.

There are disturbing parallels between the prison system and the residential schools. Many of the Indigenous people in prison are there essentially because they are Indigenous as this chapter has documented. As in the residential schools they are "out of sight," which appears to be one reason non-Indigenous Canadians know so little about them. They are subject to harsh treatment and solitary confinement. They join gangs for self-protection and may remain in those gangs after release. Their prison experience makes them poorer citizens when they emerge and perpetuates the cycle of poverty, abuse, and the revolving prison door.

On October 30, 2018, Correctional Investigator Ivan Zinger released his 2017-18 annual report on the incarceration rates of Indigenous Canadians. He found "little practical progress" in the three years since the release of the Report of the Truth and Reconciliation Commission in which 18 of the 94 Calls for Action dealt with prisons. Indigenous people made up 4.3% of the population, 28% of those in jail, and 40% of women in jail which he described as "new highs." Indigenous people still serve more of their sentences in jail than non-Indigenous ones, and more of that in higher security, situations resulting from the decisions of Corrections officials, not the courts. Corrections Canada was making less use of segregation, but the decline was 23% for non-Indigenous prisoners compared to 10% for Indigenous ones.

The government's reply was that it was doing better. Among his recommendations: "Loosening the levers and instruments of correctional (and some might say) colonial control is consistent with the path toward reconciliation between Canada and its First Nations...Of course, devolution of correctional power will only happen if there is courageous and visionary leadership at the top...supported and directed by the Government of Canada." He called for more funding, more healing lodges, better support for those released, and greater acceptance by Corrections Canada for its own responsibility "for the morass of Indigenous incarceration." His reports were reinforced by the 75-page report of the

Senate's Human Rights Committee of February 2019, entitled: "Interim Report: Study of the Human Rights of Federally-Sentenced Persons: The Most Basic Right is to be Treated as a Human Being."

Another area where there has been little progress is the use of "Gladue" reports. In 1999, the Supreme Court ruled that Indigenous Canadians faced racism in the justice system, and in making sentences, judges must consider their unique background. This was to address both the high incarceration rates and the distrust of Indigenous people in the justice system. Reports were to be prepared on each accused person that would cover matters like residential schools, foster homes, adoption, violations of hunting laws on traditional lands, language problems, and having contact with their family and community.

People were to be trained to write them, an exercise that would require obtaining the trust and cooperation of the accused. Ottawa did not draft a common form for the reports on the grounds that it is up to the provinces, and only Ontario, BC, and the Yukon developed programs to allow judges to take backgrounds into consideration. In the next two decades the proportion of Indigenous inmates in prisons continued to increase partly because Gladue reports were not being used and the system remained prejudiced against them.

The Report of the Inquiry into Missing and Murdered Indigenous Women and Girls contains two recommendations that underline the complexity of the situation First Nations face. The conditions created by a century of colonialism have led to higher incarceration rates for Indigenous people. They have also led to high rates of violence against Indigenous women by Indigenous men.

The Inquiry recommended harsher penalties for violence against Indigenous women by anyone, but one effect of that would be to keep more Indigenous men in jail for longer periods. That is a contradiction of the purpose of Gladue reports and a contradiction of the Inquiry's Calls for Action recommending greater use of Gladue reports. The recommendations were incorporated in Bill C-75 which was given Royal Assent on June 21, 2019, and which is a contradiction of government policy endorsing Gladue reports.

Fortunately, so many studies have thrown light on this crisis and so many court cases have identified human rights violations that society is moving to address the unacceptable and unjustifiable rate of incarceration of First Nations peoples. Unfortunately, the movement is so slow that the rate appears to still be on the increase. Until that changes, Canada's right to call itself a champion of human rights, racial equality, toleration and fairness will remain a myth for the non-Indigenous and a tragedy for First Nations.

Chapter 11

Welfare or Bad Fare?

"The road to hell is paved with good intentions."

By the 1950s, it was clear that the residential school system had been a dismal failure. The thousands of students who had passed through had gained some education and learned some useful trades such as farming. The schools had greater success in undermining Indigenous culture and family unity and in imposing a veneer of Christian "civilization" and beliefs on the students. But the graduates had not been assimilated. They were more likely to be sort of schizophrenic, part Indigenous and part Canadian in culture, having lost much of the best of the former and gained little of the best of the latter.

Just as decisions were being taken to phase out the failed residential schools, another far more effective method of assimilation emerged, namely adoption. Unlike the residential schools, it was not a deliberate attempt at assimilation, but it was far more effective. Provincial governments have a responsibility to society to protect children, and that is accepted by the general public, enshrined in law, and administered by departments of child welfare. If parents cannot properly look after their children or if they abuse them, the government can take them away, put them temporarily in foster families that will look after them, or have them adopted by a family that does appear to be able to provide a good permanent home and upbringing.

By the 1950s, almost a century of the policies of the Indian Act and the residential schools had produced just the type of situations in many First Nations families that child welfare agencies were designed to deal with, namely, children living in an environment of poverty, alcohol and drug abuse, and physical and sexual abuse. In 1951 the Indian Act was amended to allow provincial governments to administer child welfare on reserves on behalf of the federal government. As a result, welfare officials took children from dysfunctional families or parents, or ones deemed to be dysfunctional. Some were taken at birth from mothers assumed to be unfit or lacking the family support to look after the baby.

The children were then available for adoption. Since poverty was the lot of most First Nations, adoption meant going to non-Indigenous families. Now assimilation could be perfect because from birth or early adulthood these children would be raised in a totally non-Indigenous environment, from daybreak to nightfall, possibly with non-Indigenous brothers and sisters, hopefully surrounded by love, support, hobbies, and opportunities. They would be brown Euro-Canadians and would never know their parents or relatives or anything about their culture.

Unlike the first round of assimilation in the residential schools, this phase of assimilation was not a deliberate policy, not a conspiracy between the federal government to create the conditions that would lead to adoption and the provincial governments which would administer it. But the effect was the same as if it had been a conspiracy. In the late sixties, adoption of Indigenous children became all too common, and a new scandal in the relations between Canada and First Nations was underway.

The scandal became known as the Sixties Scoop though it started in the 50s, lasted for decades and arguably has never ended. In 1952 there were 30 Indigenous children under BC's care; a decade later there were 1,500, one-third of all children in care. The Saskatchewan Department of Welfare was the main architect of the policy as it was having to deal with a rapidly increasing number of Indigenous children. The normal solution was to put them in foster homes, but foster children had high crime rates, low education achievement, and excessive experience of child abuse, so Saskatchewan began promoting the adoption of Indigenous children by non-Indigenous families.

The program launched in 1967 was known as A.I.M, Adopt Indian Métis, other provinces followed, and programs like it have continued. In recent decades, Indigenous children have been twelve times more likely to be removed from their families as have non-Indigenous ones. On an annual basis, the number of children taken from their parents is higher than the rate of children put in residential schools at its peak level in 1953.

When the policy began there was strong opposition by First Nations who viewed it as cultural genocide. They were right - forcibly transferring children from one ethnic group to another is genocide under the UN Convention. They questioned the necessity and whether the government was making enough effort to find homes for the children on reserves or deal with the problems that made the children vulnerable. They were ignored. When adoptions were challenged in the courts, the government invariably won - after all, it was the government that made the laws, appointed the judges, operated a justice system staffed from top to bottom with non-Indigenous Canadians, and employed the expensive lawyers.

Over the next three decades some 20,000 Indigenous children were adopted, losing contact with their birth mothers and families and culture. The exact number is not known, and some were adopted abroad. Unlike many of the people who ran the residential schools, the families that adopted these children almost certainly did their best to provide a good home and did not see the process as part of a policy of assimilation.

By 2017, 18 lawsuits were underway arguing that the federal government was violating its obligations to Indigenous children by allowing these adoptions. Finally bending to the inevitable, on October 5, 2017, Ottawa settled a case that was before the Ontario Superior Court in a manner that would apply to all 18 cases. The judge found the federal government guilty of failing to prevent children from losing their Indigenous identity (cultural genocide) and from suffering psychological harm.

By the terms, the estimated 20,000 survivors who were adopted between 1951 and 1991 would receive $750M (of $1.3B originally demanded), their lawyers would receive $75M, and $50M would be used to establish a foundation for reconciliation initiatives. Minister Bennett announced it as an important step "to begin to right the wrongs." If there were over 20,000 claimants, then they would receive $25,000 each, if fewer, then up to $50,000 each. Those who accepted were barred from launching future lawsuits for other harm they might have experienced.

The agreement was confirmed at a controversial two-day hearing in Saskatoon in May 2018. One hundred survivors came. It was a public relations disaster because the meeting was intended to present details of the agreement, but the survivors thought they would also have a chance to express their feelings. Justice Michael Shore and the lawyers took an appropriate amount of time to explain matters, but survivors were limited to three minutes each which they regarded as a violation of the spirit of Reconciliation.

On November 9, a Federal Court of Appeal rejected a challenge clearing the way for payments and in late November disputes over the legal fees were settled. A major problem many survivors are facing is that records were destroyed. There were to have been three copies of each one, and they are attempting to track down copies and identify the officials who destroyed the missing ones. Survivors and the government disagree as to how much the government has done to implement recommendations that emerged from the investigations.

Psychologically closure also required that the provincial governments accept their roles. Manitoba made an official apology in June 2015, and Alberta followed in May 2018. On January 7, 2019, Premier Scott Moe delivered Saskatchewan's apology and the assurance that policies had changed, a statement that was carried on national TV. The Saskatchewan NDP, which had been the government when the program was launched, also apologized.

Immediately after the official apology, the Federation of Sovereign Indian Nations called for a moratorium on adoptions, and it was pointed out that apologies are of dubious value if the problems leading to the high numbers of First Nations in child welfare are not addressed. Information sessions were held, and 20,000 claims had been submitted by the deadline of August 31. For a variety of reasons many potential recipients had not filed claims and a request for an extension of the deadline had been made.

Indeed, the practice has not ended, and welfare services have not explained the disproportionate rate of seizure of Indigenous babies which remains 12 times the rate for non-Indigenous children. The percentage of children in welfare who are Indigenous rose from 49% to 51% between 2011 and 2016. In Manitoba 90% of children in care are Indigenous, the highest rate in Canada. One reason may be that, unlike in Ontario, when these cases come before the courts, the welfare officials do not have to produce evidence as to why they seized the child and the courts, and the government have apparently not addressed this issue.

Headlines were made in June 2019 when welfare officials in Kamloops, BC, tried to seize a baby 90 minutes after birth on the grounds that her mother was neglecting her. Two days later welfare officials removed the baby but returned her 13 days later. She was taken away again and after five weeks may be in her third or fourth home. The birth was by C-section, so the mother probably was under medication and incapable of looking after the infant. Welfare officials refused a meeting with the family because family members insisted on recording the conversation. Pam Palmater asked how a mother could be endangering her baby 90 minutes after birth and called it an example of "race-based genocide."

At the same time as the issue of the Sixties Scoop was before the courts, another case was initiated to address discrimination against First Nations children. In February 2007, Cindy Blackstock, Executive Director of the First Nations Child and Family Caring Society of Canada, joined the Assembly of First Nations in a complaint before the Canadian Human Rights Tribunal alleging that the federal government discriminated against Indigenous children by failing to provide them with the same level of welfare services as non-Indigenous children received.

Worse still, even more was needed due to the poverty rates of Indigenous people. Complaints about the quality of services for Indigenous children began to emerge in the 1970s. They reached a climax when a five-year old, Jordan Rivers Anderson, died during a two-year squabble between Ottawa and Manitoba over his expenses. The concept that governments should deal with problems first and settle accounting issues later became known as "Jordan's Principle." It applied to all services, and not just welfare, and is discussed in Chapter 14 concerning health. Implementing that Principle was the purpose of Blackstock's complaint to the HR Tribunal.

Estimates of the shortfall in federal spending compared to that of the provinces ranged from 22% to 34%, a clear case of discriminating against First Nations children. Because federal support was less than what was needed, more children were forced into the welfare system. In the court case Ottawa followed its normal practice of obstruction, but nine years later, on January 26, 2016, the Tribunal agreed in an historic and legally binding decision. The government was told to immediately "cease the discriminatory practice..." which was compared to the residential schools. It also said that First Nations should control the welfare of their children.

Manitoba Grand Chief Derek Nepinak welcomed the report saying that the Manitoba system was designed to apprehend children and that Manitoba had the highest apprehend rate in the world. The Inquiry into Missing and Murdered Women and Girls has also heard of the link between the abuse and neglect experienced in the welfare system and the number of murdered Indigenous women. Children also enter the child welfare system at a higher rate because their mothers are murdered or incarcerated at a higher rate, another vicious circle.

Justice Minister Jody Wilson-Raybould and Indigenous Affairs Minister Carolyn Bennett welcomed the report, saying it was no surprise and that the issue was about ensuring equality. Those statements begged the question: why, then, was nothing being done? Dealing with the crisis in child welfare constituted the first five Calls to Action of the 2015 Truth and Reconciliation Commission, and PM Trudeau had promised to implement all 94 of its recommendations. Bennett said that the government would soon begin working with First Nations on ways to implement the decision.

Unfortunately, that was a typical government response, the promise of discussions when the problems and solutions had been noted for decades and the issue had been before the Tribunal itself for nine years. It had ordered immediate action, not more consultations. The Ministers promised increased funding but would not say how much it would cost to close the gap though "we are going to have to significantly increase the dollars...for child welfare..." That was a fair comment at the time as the new government's spring budget was under preparation. That budget provided \$635M over five years to reform the welfare system, an amount Minister Bennett called "significant."

Cindy Blackstock pointed out that only \$71M of that \$635M was allocated for the first year and \$99M in the second and much of the commitment fell after the next election and was therefore not guaranteed. The need was \$200M annually (one billion rather than \$635M) and the government was not therefore meeting the orders of the HR Tribunal. She, the AFN and their partners went back to the Tribunal and it agreed - the government had been ordered to fix the problem "immediately" and instead was studying it and holding consultations.

In April, the Tribunal issued a non-compliance order against the government. In response, Minister Bennett said Ottawa was working with the provinces and First Nations on overhauling the system. In May, Blackstock said she had sent the government detailed recommendations for spending, but it was doing nothing. The April non-compliance order did not produce accelerated action, so in September the Tribunal issued a second one. The 2017 budget did not close the gap, and the Tribunal issued a third non-compliance order on May 26 saying little had changed and that the current government's policy was the same as that of the previous government.

While it is essential to close the gap between what is spent on Indigenous and non-Indigenous child welfare, such spending only addresses the consequences of the problem, not the problem itself, the reasons so many children must be under the care of child welfare. The conditions that produced so many First Nations children in need of welfare have never been addressed by the federal government, and they worsened after 1996 because of budget cuts. Huge numbers of First Nations children meet provincial criteria to be removed from their homes, and provincial welfare departments have been doing what is, in effect, their jobs.

In recent years the numbers of Indigenous children in provincial welfare systems has been identified as a "crisis." While they make up 8% of the Canadian population, they account for 52% of those in care, up 4% since 2011. The estimated number is 40,000, but no one knows how many there are. In Manitoba, which has the worst record, 10,000 out of 11,000 children in care are Indigenous, 6,000 of them permanent wards, an 85% increase in the last decade. In Ontario, 30% of the children in care were Indigenous, a higher proportion than went to residential schools, 2.6 times higher than their proportion of the population.

Another major problem that is now being faced is the fact that provincial child welfare agents who may correctly be removing a child from a dangerous environment may not have been diligent in determining whether relatives of that child could look after him or her. There are stories of grandparents running after the cars of welfare agents who had just taken children from homes, stories of children in foster homes spending years trying to get information on their families, running away numerous times (as happened with the residential schools), of band councils saying the children could have been looked after on the reserve. As with so many of these issues, one factor seems to be the desire of civil servants to exercise power, a desire reflected in a reluctance to listen to advice.

Part of the problem is dysfunctional federalism. The Manitoba government is now spending around $500M annually on child welfare, 90% of which is for First Nations people. That is to deal with problems caused by the fact that the federal government is not spending enough on reserves to deal with poverty. As the two levels of government manoeuvre, grapple with problems, defend their interests and power, and play the blame-game, tax dollars are wasted, problems go unsolved, and the problems within the child care system help produce crime, drug and alcohol abuse, high incarceration rates, and murdered and missing women and girls, all of which add to the costs of government, federal, provincial, municipal, and reserve. And to the cost of child welfare.

On January 25-26, 2018, the second anniversary of HR Tribunal's order, Jane Philpott who had been appointed Minister of Indigenous Services five months earlier, hosted a major meeting in Ottawa with all the stakeholders to examine the overall problem and reach some agreements on how to tackle it. In an unusual step, she preceded the meeting with a press conference in which she stated that Indigenous childcare was in "crisis" and documented their terrible plight, that is, the abject failure of her own and previous federal governments. Philpott promised full implementation of the HR Tribunal's order.

The meeting was a public relations success with much praise for the new, open, and energetic Minister. The meeting was viewed as somewhat of a new departure, a federal government that was actually listening and seeking to create consensus, abandoning the colonial attitude that "Ottawa knows best." Minister Philpott outlined several federal initiatives to implement the orders of the HR Tribunal; shift the program focus to prevention; support communities to redraw areas of jurisdiction; support Inuit and Métis leaders on culturally appropriate child and family services; and develop a data and reporting strategy.

AFN Grand Chief Bellegarde pointed out that it did not produce what he wanted to see, namely an action plan. Cindy Blackstock said there had been inquiries and recommendations for decades and that there was no reason government could not be taking the actions everyone knew needed to be taken. "We're going to go over there and talk about the same recommendations that have been on the books for 20 or 30 years..." More consultations like this one was what Bennett had promised two years earlier when the Tribunal first reported, and it was suggested that there would have been little progress if the Tribunal had not issued its original order and the following three non-compliance orders.

Minister Philpott also said the funding gap would be addressed in the next budget but gave no details. The following week the HR Tribunal issued its fourth non-compliance order because the government had still not responded to the order to close the gap "immediately." Minister Philpott replied that the government had been working closely with all parties to implement the Tribunal's orders, paying more costs, and reforming the system, and that the 2018 budget would add more money.

The 2018 budget provided \$1.4B in additional spending over five years, close to \$300M a year. Minister Philpott later said the government had thus met the Tribunal's orders, but Blackstock corrected her because putting figures in a budget was not the same as spending the money and spending it properly. In September, it was announced that after a year of consultations, Ottawa had reached agreement with the three national Indigenous organizations to spend \$1.7B over ten years on childcare. This would raise annual spending from \$500M to \$870M and reduce the number of children in foster care. The announcement was warmly welcomed by Indigenous leaders. But the Trudeau government is also reported to have spent \$700,000 in legal fees fighting the Human Rights Tribunal on this issue.

The agreement required devolving the administration of child welfare to First Nations. In late 2018 the DIA was busy drafting the necessary legislation with a view to tabling it in Parliament in late January. At that time Minister Philpott said that the real challenge was reducing the numbers apprehended, that the bill would be a "turning point." The replacement of Indigenous Services Minister Jane Philpott by Seamus O'Regan on January 14 was not well received given his less-than-stellar performance in the less-demanding portfolio of Veterans Affairs.

By mid-February, draft legislation had been circulated to Indigenous groups and the provinces. Ottawa claimed that the legislation reflected consultations; Indigenous groups said that the legislation was not acceptable unless it devolved control of child welfare to them and provided adequate funding, and the legislation did not clearly do either. The funding question involves confirming in legislation that Indigenous children will receive services equal to those provided to non-Indigenous ones. Indigenous leaders claimed that the government had not given a clear answer to the question of who would retain jurisdiction and that the provinces were blocking the legislation over the issue because they would lose control over the system and the resources. A frustrated First Nations Chief Perry Bellegarde wrote PM Trudeau urging him to personally intervene "as a litmus test of your political will to finally break from generations of colonial policies…"

On February 28 the government tabled Bill C-92, the long-awaited reform to child welfare. In principle, it is a revolutionary document. The federal government would take control of Indigenous children child welfare back from the provinces and pass it to band councils, a further step in increasing Indigenous self-government. Many good principles were incorporated: first priority would be to find relatives who could look after the child, the second would be to find other members of the community, and siblings were to be kept together. The problems that push so many Indigenous children into welfare will be addressed with programs for teen parents, drugs, and so forth. Culture will be given consideration, as well as the child's views and needs. Criteria for taking children such as overcrowding in housing were to be abolished as the solution to that lay with housing, not welfare.

Each First Nation was to draft a program and have 12 months to work out an agreement to implement it with Ottawa and the relevant province. If there was no agreement within 12 months, their program would come into effect and supersede federal and provincial law "if reasonable efforts" had been made to reach agreement. If Ottawa and the provinces define "reasonable efforts", then they have vetoes.

Problems were immediately identified. The Bill does not transfer control of First Nations children to Indigenous governments. It does not contain a guarantee of funding. It will be based on individual agreements which could lead to inequalities. It does not guarantee that the provinces will abandon control, power and budgets for a large portion of their huge welfare programs to Indigenous peoples. The program assumes the other causes of the welfare crisis – housing, health, infrastructure, drugs and so forth will be addressed, the same list of inadequacies identified in the Report of the Commission into Missing and Murdered Indigenous Women and Girls and in numerous other reports. Principles like the "child's best interests" are suspect as they were also the basis of the residential schools and the Sixties Scoop, and the legislation does not confirm that First Nations alone will determine their children's best interests.

Some First Nations supported the Bill but requested changes; the Assembly of Manitoba Chiefs opposed it from the beginning. As late as May a dozen Chiefs from western Canada were calling for protests to oppose the Bill. Other protests in Winnipeg centered on the lack of consultations and other problems. Frustration with the lack of progress led to the tabling on March 5 of a $3.0B class action suit against Ottawa for discrimination on the grounds of systematically underfunding First Nations child welfare. It covers the period from 1991 to 2019 and argues that Ottawa knew for years that there were "severe inadequacies" in its funding. It remains to be seen how many of the affected individuals will join the class action and how it will fare in the courts. The Bill was passed in June and it will take at least a year to determine whether it can be implemented, with proper funding and the agreement and cooperation of the provinces. In 2020 it will remain a very important "work in progress."

Meanwhile, progress is being made on the provincial front. One of the many problems is that funding is allocated to the agencies based on the number of children and the length of stay in the system. That gives a perverse incentive to those managing the system to maximize the number of children seized, keep them as long as possible, and make the least effort to find alternative solutions within their communities. That only reinforces the natural tendency of any bureaucracy to grow and maximize salaries, promotions, benefits, and power.

On February 11 the Manitoba government announced that it was shifting to a block-granting system which addresses that problem. It will also delegate more authority to the agencies which matches the goals of the federal government. While welcomed, Indigenous organizations pointed out that this could be a cost-saving measure in disguise, did not address the main issue of devolving jurisdiction, and did not reflect adequate consultations. Manitoba is also examining the correlation between child welfare and incarceration rates: 90% of the youth in jail are Indigenous and 60% of youths charged with crimes had been in the child welfare system. That is no surprise, but some good might come from the study.

But four years into the Trudeau government's mandate and three and a half years after the Tribunal's initial decision the problem had still not been addressed. On September 6, 2019, a seemingly exasperated Canadian Human Rights Tribunal ordered the federal government to pay $40,000 for each child affected (possibly as many as 80,000), plus $20,000 to each parent or grandparent who was a primary caregiver and another $20,000 to them for each child taken. It said: "Canada was aware of the discrimination and of the serious consequences..." and that Canada's actions were "willful and reckless..."

Cindy Blackstock said the ruling indicates that the government learned nothing from the residential school disaster and that piecemeal approaches did not work. Mary Ellen Turpel-Lafond, child advocate in BC, said the government had fought the issue every step of the way up to the present. Minister O'Regan issued a statement saying the government had doubled spending on child and family services. That was instructive as the Tribunal's 2016 order was that it end discrimination immediately by closing the gap on what is spent on First Nations and non-Indigenous children, and it clearly does not believe the government has done that.

Progress is definitely being made but Canada is only just beginning to grapple with the problems created by the serious underfunding of First Nations child welfare not to mention the conditions that put so many First Nations children at risk.

Chapter 12

Missing and Murdered but not Forgotten

Murder has been an unfortunate aspect of human behaviour since before the dawn of civilization and all societies develop means to control it. Sometimes the victim's body is not found so the incident is listed as "missing," but with rare exceptions, "missing" means murdered but not found. Any murder rate is unacceptable, but in Canada, estimates for the rate of missing and murdered Indigenous women and girls over the past four decades vary between three and seven times those for non-Indigenous women. In some provinces, the rate is ten times that for others. For decades here have been demands for an inquiry. Interestingly, during the past two decades almost no Canadians have died as a result of terrorist attacks. Billions of dollars have been spent fighting terrorism, an amount out of all proportion to that spent dealing with murdered Indigenous women.

This chapter will examine the many aspects of this serious issue. However, while attention is focussed on the tragedy of women, First Nations males suffer murder rates far above those of non-Indigenous Canadians, possibly higher than the rate for women. Infamous examples include the "starlight rides" in which inadequately clothed men were taken by the police to the outskirts of western Canadian cities in the dead of winter where they froze to death. A study done by APTN indicated that in Winnipeg there were 119 murders between 2014 and 2018 – 36 were Indigenous men, 20 were Indigenous women. The high number of male deaths in police custody is a continuing problem. Men also suffer physical and sexual abuse. It is not entirely clear why the attention was focussed so overwhelmingly on women when the problem of violence against Indigenous people can hardly be addressed when half or more of the victims are left out of the study.

Though it has received considerable publicity in the last decade, the problem of missing and murdered Indigenous women is not new. First Nations have been calling attention to it for decades. The Manitoba Aboriginal Justice Inquiry of 1991 recommended changes but they were not implemented. The RCMP report of May 2014 came as a shock because it said there were almost 1,200 cases of missing and murdered women and girls from 1980 to 2012, more than twice the previous estimate, plus about another 200 dating back to 1952. That statistic only covered the ones officially reported on police files, an obvious underestimate of the real number. The government hinted that the majority were killed by Aboriginal people but the RCMP has no reliable definition of Aboriginal people.

A 2015 UN report said that Indigenous women were five times more likely to die violently than non-Indigenous ones. A Statistics Canada report of 2014 said that Indigenous women were 2.7 times as likely to face violence and that the proportion of female victims who are Indigenous increased from 9% of female homicides in 1980 to 24% in 2015. In BC, the Highway of Tears between Prince Rupert and Prince George is well known, a stretch of road where hitch-hiking is common as is the disappearance of First Nations women. In Vancouver, Robert Picton murdered Indigenous women for years, the police mishandling of that shameful episode leading to the Oppal Inquiry of 2010. These figures are almost certainly underestimated because data has not been properly collected, a fact which itself calls into question the attitude of authorities.

Individual cases have been covered in the media for decades. A famous one involved Betty Osborne, a young Cree woman in The Pas, Manitoba, who was brutally raped and murdered on November 13, 1971. The police concentrated on possible First Nations perpetrators but probably knew within a year that was not likely, and like so many similar cases, the file went cold. Sixteen years later, a newly arrived policeman placed an ad in the paper asking for information. This led to the identification of four suspects who seem to have been known to many people, and one of them was convicted in December 1987. The case led to widespread discussion of racism and discrimination and on July 14, 2000, the Government of Manitoba formally apologized for the failure of its justice system. Eight years later Osborne's brother was murdered in Winnipeg.

Little has changed. On January 10, 2015, Nadine Machiskinic, fell 10 stories down a laundry chute in the Delta Hotel in Regina, dying from her injuries. Two years later the Regina Police asked the RCMP to investigate because of growing criticism of its handling of the case. The

RCMP reported in early 2018. Regina Police Chief Evan Bray said the report would not be released but then had to release it in March 2019 under an access to information request.

It was a scathing indictment of failure to follow proper procedure. Her cell phone was not checked for over two weeks. Surveillance tapes were not requested for ten days, by which time they had been destroyed, and a toxicology report was not requested for four months. It was over a year before the hotel guest list was obtained, and no one seemed to have taken control of the investigation. The RCMP said the Regina Police failed to meet "the standards of a professional, sudden death investigation," but Police Chief Evan Bray said: "I remain confident that...it was thoroughly investigated." The coroner said the cause of death was undetermined and later changed that to accidental, but the jury at the coroner's inquest changed it back to undetermined.

For decades First Nations and others demanded a national inquiry into the overall issue. There were three elements to the demand. One was for an opportunity for the relatives and friends of victims to express their feelings publicly in order to obtain some psychological closure, for "shedding their trauma or sharing their pain." Another was to obtain a better understanding as to why so little had been done to solve these cases and prevent others. The third was to provide a set of recommendations to deal with the problem. The Harper Conservative government refused to appoint an inquiry arguing that there had been enough inquiries (almost 100) and what was needed was tougher action against the perpetrators.

In the 2015 federal election campaign Liberal leader Justin Trudeau promised to appoint an inquiry. The promise was accepted as genuine even by those who had witnessed and experienced decades of broken promises and knew the sad history of government policy dating back to the Indian Act. Within months, however, questions began to arise about the government's sincerity and its ability to turn its promise into the meaningful inquiry so long demanded. Since then the Inquiry has been the subject of controversy, administrative chaos, resignations, criticism, extreme disappointment, calls for a complete re-start, and buck-passing over the reasons for its problems.

The new Liberal government announced in December the beginning of consultations to determine the objectives, focus and parameters of the inquiry. It was to be established in the spring of 2016, but the Commissioners were not named until August and the Inquiry did not begin work until September. The mandate was: "to examine the systemic causes of all forms of violence against Indigenous women, girls and of the LGBTQ2S community in Canada." The Inquiry was given a two-year mandate with a final report due on December 31, 2018, a very short period given the magnitude of the problem and compared to other inquiries. The selection of the Commissioners drew criticism. Chief Commissioner Marion Buller had many excellent qualifications but lacked experience in administration and as a judge had not been allowed to deal with the media. Administration and public relations became problem areas.

The bureaucracy did not appear to treat the establishment of the inquiry as a priority. It took months to find office space. It was given out-of-date computers and had problems communicating over five time zones. Reimbursing staff and witness expenses and paying salaries was botched and delays were frequent and unexplained. Phones were not answered, calls not returned. The Inquiry has had problem contacting families but rejected offers by both AFN and Native Women's Association of Canada to use their sophisticated contact systems.

The mandate was not sufficiently clear, and Commissioner Buller did not impose a clear direction, set of objectives, road map, or timetable. The Inquiry's plan was established as it went along and interested parties could not obtain information as to what was happening next or when. The lack of direction was actually confirmed by Commissioner Buller in an interview with CBC on April 8, 2018: "I think the best way of explaining it is we had to design the car, build the car, and then drive the car all at the same time." That is not how inquiries are done, and someone noted that it is a recipe for an accident.

From the beginning questions arose as to whether the inquiry would seriously look at the role of the police, or lack thereof, in dealing with the murders. In July 2017, the Inquiry said it would consider the conduct of the police. This was regarded by some as an expansion of its mandate, and not just a clarification. In its November 2017, Interim Report, the Inquiry said the study of the role of the police was a "centrepiece" of its work, but it did not begin to subpoena records for 10 months. By January 2018, it had not yet started examining the police files because it still lacked the technology to read them. As of February 2018, the police in eight major cities said that they had not been contacted. By the time its authority to subpoena documents expired, it had only contacted 28 police forces. By April 2019 only 174 of the 479 files requested had arrived. Many files from the RCMP were useless because they were so heavily redacted and the RCMP argued that some files could not be produced until long after the Inquiry wrapped up.

The Inquiry was a major issue at a meeting of the Assembly of First Nations in late July 2017. There the Chiefs called for major changes, to make it more transparent and less legalistic, to give the participants more input into how it operates, to obtain more funding, and to extend the mandate. Manitoba Grand Chief Sheila North-Wilson asked for the federal government to intervene - she had previously called on all the Commissioners to resign. A vote calling for a "hard reset" failed to pass but indicated widespread concern with the Inquiry.

Throughout its existence the Inquiry was plagued by personnel issues, tensions, infighting, resignations, dismissals, and gaps in staffing. Over a dozen major members of the Inquiry had resigned by January 2018 plus half a dozen lawyers. Their complaints, including one letter to the Prime Minister, covered a wide variety of serious concerns: leadership, organization, confusion, the mandate, insufficient time, the process, lack of transparency, disrespect for participants, difficulty dealing with the government, problems with reimbursements, lack of independence, political interference, a colonial or top-down process, and the fact that many of these factors were connected.

By the summer of 2017, Commissioners were musing publicly about the need for an extension and for a substantial increase in funding, but it was only on March 6, 2018, that Buller made the request. Three months later the government agreed to a six-month extension, to April 30, 2019, and the budget was increased by \$38M for a total of \$92M. Minister Bennett pointed out that there was no consensus amongst the provinces for a further extension, an interesting argument since both crime and Indian affairs are federal responsibilities.

On November 1, 2017, the Commission issued an Interim Report with 10 recommendations. At the same time as the announcement of the extension, Minister Bennett announced the government's response to some of the recommendations in the Inquiry's Interim Report. The response included $21.3M for health services to the families of survivors, a commemorative fund of $10M, $5.2M for family liaison units, and $9.6M for the new RCMP unit to deal with unsolved cases. By the end of the process 2,380 people including 468 family members and survivors had spoken. Prime Minister Trudeau did honour the promise to establish an Inquiry, but it was a text-book case on how not to do it.

Perhaps typical of this and the previous government's mishandling of this entire issue is the program to support Parents of Missing or Murdered Children (PMMC). It was launched by the Conservative government on January 1, 2013, to help roughly 1,000 families deal with their trauma and provided potentially $350 per week for 35 weeks. Unfortunately, it was poorly designed, poorly advertised, and had an overly complicated application process. Eligibility criteria discouraged parents from taking advantage as they could not be employed or be receiving EI and had to apply within one year of the child's murder or disappearance.

In August 2017, the Ombudsman for the Victims of Crime, Sue O'Sullivan, issued a scathing indictment of the program. In the first three years of its operation, only $223,000 had been paid out of a budget of $33M. That was 0.5% of the money available while administrative costs were 14 times as much as payouts. Following that report the federal government promised changes but the problems were not fixed and in the following year payments actually declined.

In April 2018, Dubravka Simonovic, the UN Special Rapporteur on violence against women, made a 13-day visit to Canada. She reported that Indigenous women face marginalization, exclusion and poverty because of institutional, systemic, multiple, intersecting forms of discrimination that have not been addressed adequately by the government. She repeated the basic facts that have been known for years, that Indigenous women are assaulted three times more often than non-Indigenous ones, face eight times the rate of domestic violence, and are seven times as likely to be murdered by a serial killer. She said that in addition to appointing the Inquiry, Canada had to address the root causes of violence which could be done right away. "It is not sufficient to work only on one issue...What I am seeing is only (an) inquiry process..."

The lack of confidence in the Inquiry was reflected in the fact that in July 2018, a First Nations woman, Diane BigEagle, launched a $600M class-action lawsuit against the RCMP on behalf of all families who had members whose murder or disappearance had been reported to the RCMP. The RCMP are accused of mishandling cases and systemic negligence, discrimination, and of being influenced by overt and covert racism. Because of that, criminals allegedly do not fear prosecution and that increases the violence against Indigenous women. These cases are having some effect, and on June 25, 2018, the new Commissioner of the RCMP, Brenda Lucki, apologized to families of murdered and missing women saying the RCMP could have done better and now has better training and more cultural awareness. Commissioner Buller thought the apology was sincere; First Nations spokespersons indicated they would judge the RCMP by its actions, not its words. Winnipeg Police Chief Danny Smyth apologized for the treatment of Indigenous women in his city and Royal Newfoundland Constabulary Chief Joe Boland acknowledged his department's failures and the need to build trust.

On June 5, 2019, the Inquiry issued its 1,200-page Report. It had ultimately heard over 2,300 witnesses. It made 231 recommendations (48 pages) or "Calls for Justice" which are labelled "legal imperatives," that is, orders to governments and others. They address all the factors that lead to murder, to inadequate investigation of murder or that could make Indigenous women and girls more vulnerable to violence than non-Indigenous ones. Basically, they include solving all the problems identified in this book. Problems in policing and the justice system are part of the problem so governments must fix them: reform the RCMP, better training, better prison conditions. Poor conditions on reserves drive women into dangerous situations so governments must fix them: poverty, unemployment, infrastructure, housing, transportation, education, welfare, even declining language capacity.

The Inquiry's mandate did not include examining cold cases but it recommends that they be re-opened. There should be no more adoption by non-Indigenous families and welfare should be under the control of Indigenous people. All Canadians should learn their history and fight racism. There should be self-determination, self-government, more Indigenous people in every sector of society dealing with Indigenous people. Many of the Calls for Justice are for activities governments are already doing and may have been pursuing for decades – the Call is to move faster. It hardly needs saying that most of the recommendations also apply to Indigenous males.

There are contradictions in the Calls for Justice. It recommends greater use of Gladue Reports which are designed to ensure that the justice system takes account of an Indigenous person's history. That means, for example, that being a residential school survivor may explain conduct and suggest a more lenient sentence. But harsher sentencing is also recommended for those who attack Indigenous women and girls. That would increase the incarceration rate of Indigenous males while the Report recommends that the high incarceration rate of Indigenous females be addressed. Stiffer sentences for violent crimes was one of the most criticized aspects of the Harper government's policy towards Indigenous people.

The Report was immediately immersed in controversy because it called the tragedy "genocide." Attention focussed on the appropriateness and significance of that word. The acts themselves meet four of the UN's criteria for genocide, but not that of deliberate "intent" by the government to eliminate an entire ethnic group. The accusation is extremely serious because if the Canadian state committed genocide, then it could be taken to the international court in The Hague as other states have been. Because the Report did not recommend that, the impression was left that it had just used the word for effect. And if there was genocide, it was against men as well as women. The result, however, was that attention focussed on the use of the word "genocide" rather than on the Calls for Justice. Indeed, the inappropriateness became evident when the Organization of American States indicated that it wanted to investigate the matter.

The word "genocide" caused confusion in the government. At the release ceremony PM Trudeau did not acknowledge the use of the word but the next day he did which presumably meant that he accepted that Canada could be tried for the crime at The Hague. Leader of the Opposition Andrew Scheer said the tragedy did not meet the criteria for genocide. A Leger poll showed 53% agreeing that the tragedy was genocide, 34% disagreeing, but no agreement on what acts constituted genocide or who was responsible. The debate diverted attention from the Calls for Action themselves and opinion was divided as to whether the use of the word helped or hindered the cause of reducing the victimization of Indigenous women and girls. In *The Sleeping Giant* Professor David Macdonald argues persuasively that what happened to First Nations over 150 years, the starvation, residential schools, adoption and sterilization, does meet the criteria of genocide. In 1919 the Canadian Museum for Human Rights finally acknowledged that the 150 years of colonialism was genocide and not just cultural genocide as it had previously argued.

The Inquiry into Missing and Murdered Women and Girls definitely raised awareness of all the problems that led to this tragedy and still do. It will almost certainly add to the momentum to deal with the problems that have been known for a century. But while the Inquiry carried on, Indigenous women and girls continued to be murdered or go missing at a far higher rate than others.

An organization called Families of Sisters in Spirit (FSIS) has been compiling a list of Indigenous women murdered or having suspicious deaths since 2015. The count is 140 or 45 per year but does not include those missing. The 2014 RCMP report estimated 1,181 between 1980 and 2012 or roughly 65 per year, but that figure included missing women. If those missing over the past three years are added to the figure of140, there may have been no decline at all and there may have been an increase. The data base of Sovereign Bodies indicates 131 since 2015 – both suggest no decline in spite of the publicity provided by the Inquiry and whatever additional effort has been made by police and governments over the past four years.

None of these figures are accurate. Indeed, some of statistics in the final Report were wildly inaccurate. It said Indigenous females accounted for 25% of homicides when the real figure is around 6%, an exaggeration of 400% which indicates an appalling lack of care and proof-reading by all those involved in a $90M inquiry of such importance. That was not the only error: a corrected (but not explained) electronic version was issued but the original electronic and hard-copy versions were not recalled. The overall picture is clear, however: there has been little change. The recommendations of past inquiries have not been implemented, the problems have not been addressed, the people responsible for the failures have not been held accountable, and not much changed while the Inquiry was holding its hearings.

Then, in November 2018, a new form of "missing and murdered" gained prominence when Métis Senator Yvonne Boyer used her first speech in the Senate to highlight the fact that for decades Indigenous women have been experiencing sterilization that was arguably coerced, that is, with permission obtained under pressure when they were giving birth. No living persons were "missing or murdered," but future children were. Concerns about alleged forced sterilization had been given to the TRC. Two of the victims launched a lawsuit in 2017 against the Saskatoon Health Region and the federal and provincial governments. Sixty other victims joined the lawsuit and another 32 came forward after news items appeared in November. In December 2018, another lawsuit for $500M was launched against the government of Alberta regarding unapproved sterilizations dating back to 1977.

Indigenous Services Minister Jane Philpott said the practice must stop; the Canadian Press report of November 12, 2018, said it was continuing. In March a new case in Saskatchewan dating from December 13, 2018, was reported to the Senate committee. Concerns were expressed by the AFN, Amnesty International Canada, the federal NDP, and Senator Murray Sinclair. Forced sterilization is a violation of the United Nations Convention on the Prevention of Genocide (preventing births within a group), and the United Nations Committee Against Torture told Canada to stop the practice in November 2018.

It gave Canada a year to report. That Committee recommended that Canada criminalize involuntary sterilization, a recommendation the AFN supported. Ottawa replied that existing law was adequate. However, when the above-mentioned new case was reported to Minister Ralph Goodale's office, it referred to forced sterilization as a "serious violation of human rights," not as a crime. Calls were made for investigations of all such recent cases.

In early 2019 talks were proceeding between federal and provincial authorities and the House of Commons was examining the issue. A House of Commons Committee was also studying the issue and released its report in August. It called on the government to launch an immediate investigation because forced sterilizations were still being carried out. Minister O'Regan's office issued a statement saying the practice was "deeply troubling" and urging alleged victims to go to the police. The Commons Committee had already heard from experts saying that the women involved did not trust the RCMP.

In February NDP MP Don Davies formally asked the RCMP to launch a criminal investigation and lay any appropriate charges. The RCMP replied on March 20 saying that a preliminary review of their data revealed no evidence of complaints. The College of Physicians and Surgeons of Ontario said the reports were "troubling." Both the House of Commons and the Senate have appointed committees to study the situation.

One issue that emerges repeatedly with these cases is that of the police investigating themselves, a practice they say is quite satisfactory, a practice First Nations find unacceptable. A variation is for one police force to investigate incidents involving another which, for First Nations, is roughly the same. The issue was back in the news in Saskatoon in July 2019, after the release of a corner's inquest into the 2016 shooting of Joshua Megeney. The lawyer representing the family questioned how the public could have confidence in the investigation by the police themselves and recommended that such investigations had to be done by independent civilian bodies, a recommendation that seems to be gaining support.

One is reminded of the outrageously funny history of England "*1066 and All That*." The basis of British democracy is the Magna Carta of 1215 in which English nobles forced King John to accept the concept of trial by peers. The account in "*1066 and All That*" describes it thusly: Nobles shall be tried by nobles because they understand. In Canada, it appears that policemen who kill First Nations are investigated by policemen "because they understand." First Nations people who kill non-Indigenous Canadians are tried by non-Indigenous juries, not by their peers, that is, by juries of Indigenous Canadians. Two days after the release of the Inquiry's Report, Public Safety Minister Ralph Goodale announced the makeup of an advisory board to oversee the RCMP, a body independent of the RCMP that can receive and investigate complaints. No Indigenous women were included.

Chapter 13

Water, water everywhere, Nor any drop to drink

In 1834, Samuel Taylor Coleridge wrote the above line in his famous poem "The Rime of the Ancient Mariner," but it is a good description of the water situation on many of Canada's reserves in 2019. When Europeans arrived in North America, people could probably drink water from almost every lake, river and stream from coast to coast. Four hundred years later, the CBC reported that in the decade from 2005 to 2015, two thirds of Canada's reserves had problems with their drinking water. In Saskatchewan, the figure was 93%. On one reserve in Ontario the residents had been boiling their water for 20 years. The reserves include ones beside non-Indigenous communities that have clean water and ones beside pristine lakes in remote regions of the country. Surprisingly perhaps, the number was still increasing and at any given time, one-quarter of reserves could be under at least one boil-water advisory. Canada has almost one fifth of the world's fresh water, but it is not very fresh on reserves.

There are problems with every type of infrastructure on reserves - housing, health facilities, firefighting equipment, schools, roads, and water. Measuring something like housing is difficult because "substandard" is a subjective term and changes from decade to decade, between provinces, and whenever new regulations are introduced. The quality of roads or education is also difficult to compare precisely. But water either can or cannot be consumed and, for washing, either is or is not clear. The measure of whether it is safe is whether it is under a boil-water advisory which are science-based reports issued by Health Canada.

The number of such advisories is posted on the website but there are difficulties using the information as found in articles and statements. There are several types of advisories and the ones usually quoted are those in place for over a year, the serious ones. A reserve could have some safe sources of water and some sources under advisories. Figuring out how much money Ottawa spends dealing with water problems on reserves is a challenge. Most figures found in articles cover both water supply and wastewater management, with about 60% of the amount being for water supply. Amounts are often given as X dollars over Y years, but spending is usually low in the first few years as the program ramps up. Some figures are for capital investment alone and do not include maintenance or training, and the money could come from various governments and departments. The literature on spending on water problems is thus a jumble of contradictory figures and timeframes. They paint a clear picture of inadequacy, but how inadequate is difficult to tell.

Boil-water advisories result from impurities or bacteria in the water, corroded pipes and connections, and breakdowns in the water treatment plants. The latter results from lack of spare parts, training or basic information such as manuals. On some reserves running water can only be used for washing but that is discouraging for human hygiene if the water is coloured and destructive for washing clothes if too much chlorine has been added. In addition, some houses are not connected to the water supply and obtain their water by truck or bottle. DIA and Health Canada do not ensure regular testing of water quality on reserves. Drinking water is tested properly in municipalities, a double standard pointed out by Human Rights Watch on June 7, 2017. But even when water is pure at the treatment plant, it may not be safe to drink in a house. Many houses are not connected to the treatment plant, so water is stored in cisterns, and if they are not cleaned regularly, the pure water will become contaminated. Those situations are not recorded in the boil-water advisories.

The result for those who do consume contaminated water are predictable: diarrhea, gastrointestinal illnesses, infections, rapid spread of infections and diseases, a slow rate of healing, skin rashes, and poor hygiene. Clothes turn brown or deteriorate due to the excessive use of chlorine. Deaths have been attributed to water quality. One of the worst examples was an outbreak of E.coli on the Kashechewan Reserve in northern Ontario in 2005 which led to the evacuation by air of 1,000 people. These conditions are depressing, and depression is a factor in drug and alcohol abuse. There is considerable debate about the root causes of the situation, but one aspect is clear. In every aspect of reserve life - water treatment, health, education, housing, infrastructure - the federal government has spent substantially less per capita than provincial governments and municipal have spent on the same matters for non-Indigenous Canadians.

A 2011 assessment of 571 reserves with a total population of almost 500,000 found that 39% of the water systems were at a high risk of having poor water quality and 34% were at medium risk. Only 54% had fully qualified technicians. The cost of fixing the problems was estimated at $850M plus over $800M annually for maintenance. Another report estimated that two billion dollars had been spent annually between 2001 and 2013 during which time the number of advisories increased.

Water management seems to provide a microcosm of what is wrong with Ottawa's overall handling of reserves. Canadian municipalities are responsible for supplying clean water to citizens and businesses, and if there is a problem, it is clear who is responsible, and it is fixed as quickly as possible. It is impossible to imagine a municipality going without clean drinking water for weeks let alone years or two decades as in the case of one reserve. When a large mineral deposit is discovered the company does not delay development for years waiting for the water treatment plant to be built even if it is a few kilometers from a reserve that has not had clean drinking water for years. The same is true of government facilities such as dams or military bases - the water plants get built quickly and maintained properly.

Unlike the municipality, military base or the company town, responsibility for clean water on reserves is divided. As with almost everything to do with First Nations, real power rests with the DIA so non-Indigenous civil servants in Ottawa are really in charge. Part of that power is delegated to reserve councils, but they do not have the power or money to maintain their water treatment plants. The literature mentions plants not being built, pipes not being installed or maintained, spare parts and manuals not being provided or being out of date, personnel not being trained, and perhaps most importantly, decisions not being made, and amazingly, money not being spent.

The result is that equipment wears out quickly due to poor maintenance and operation. DIA has built plants that never worked properly. In some cases, boil-water advisories had to be maintained after millions were spent repairing a plant. Plants were built and repaired without adequate supervision. Some plants are too small for the communities. One commentator said it takes longer for DIA to approve a system than it takes to build it, that there were layers of bureaucracy designed to slow the process because there is not enough money to build the plants according to schedules.

One factor is that warnings about problems and potential problems are not coordinated between different agencies, not provided on a regular basis, and often not acted on. In addition to local authorities and observers, three federal departments are involved in flagging immediate and potential problems - DIA, Health, and Environment, but only one, DIA is involved in addressing them. It pays 80% of the cost, the reserve the other 20% but the reserve may not be able to provide its 20%. If the project is delayed, inflation pushes the cost up. As money is wasted through lack of maintenance, costs mount and consume a larger share of the budget. Trucking or flying in water also adds to cost and the use of plastic containers adds to pollution.

One of the most paradoxical situations concerns Shoal Lake near the Manitoba-Ontario border. In 1919, the city of Winnipeg built a 150-km aqueduct from the lake. It was a marvel of engineering, optimism and foresight, with the capacity to service a population of a million which Winnipeg has still not reached. But in 2017, all seven treatment plants on the reserve on that lake had been under advisories for 20 years. In September 2019 construction began on a treatment plant that is to be completed by December 2020. Another paradox: in July 2019 residents of the Thames First Nation were being told to conserve water while swimming pool hours on neighbouring municipalities were being extended.

Many of the reasons given for the situation are, in fact, excuses. These include the fact that many reserves are small, in remote areas, have difficult geography, cannot control off-reserve sources of contaminants, rest on permafrost, or the people have unique cultures different from those on other reserves. But all these factors apply to other communities in remote areas where the citizens do have clean drinking water. An interesting excuse, often repeated, is that in remote communities, equipment has to be delivered on ice highways in the winter. That would explain the first delay, not twenty. Perhaps the worst excuse ever provided was that poor water resulted from beaver dams, things First Nations had lived with for 12,000 years and which were, in fact, part of their management of the dry prairie ecosystems.

During the 2015 federal election campaign, Liberal leader Justin Trudeau promised to ensure that all reserves had clean drinking water by March 2021. In January of 2015 there were 169 advisories on 126 reserves covering 20% of the total reserve population. A report commissioned months earlier by DIA said that it would cost $4.7B over 10 years to fix the problem. Spending in the previous five-year period had been $2.2B and the 2016 budget allocated an additional $1.8B over five years which would bring the total to $4.0B. But on December 7, 2017, the Parliamentary Budget Office (PBO) issued a report stating that the government's estimate was 30% short of what was needed, which they estimated to be an additional $3.2B. The PBO felt the government had underestimated population growth and it also pointed out that the Liberal plan did not cover all reserves.

In December 2017, Minister Jane Philpott said 29 long-term advisories had been lifted since the election but another ten had been added and 67 were then in place, a net reduction of ten. In January 2018, that figure jumped to 91, an increase resulting from DIA taking responsibility for 250 systems that had previously not been counted. On July 17, 2018, the Health Canada website indicated that since 2015, 67 advisories had been lifted but 34 new ones added for a total of 72.

One example is informative. The oldest advisory is on the Neskantage Reserve near Attawapiskaat and dates from 1995 where the water is drawn from a bog rather than the nearby river. In December 2015, Ottawa promised a new treatment plant by late spring, 2018, but it was then delayed until March 2019. In February 2019 the band council fired the construction company and took over the project. On July 7 the council declared a state of emergency over the quality of water.

The residents demanded that the Canadian Armed Forces send the Disaster Assistance Response Team. Ottawa promised to send a health official in a few days because, as a spokesperson said: "Its for sure a top priority, that is why we are acting very quickly on this." Minister O'Regan visited and promised a quick fix but it was clear the residents no longer believe federal promises. North of Thunder Bay the Eabametoong Fist Nation declared a state of emergency on July 15, 2019 – they have had to boil their water for 18 years. Minister O'Regan promised to speak to reserve leaders soon.

Progress is definitely being made and the media carries reports of the lifting of advisories in various provinces. In July 2018, the Semiahmoo First Nations signed a deal with the neighbouring City of Surrey, BC, that will bring clean water to the reserve in the spring of 2019 and allow the installation of fire hydrants. The negotiations for that began in the 1970s and the reserve was under an advisory for 15 years. Beside Edmonton the 25-year-old advisory on the Enoch Cree Reserve was lifted in March 2019, but water is still distributed by truck.

However, there is little sign that DIA is willing to give reserves complete responsibility and adequate funding for water treatment and put them on an equal administrative basis with municipalities, so the fundamental political and administrative problem remains unresolved with civil servants in Ottawa micro-managing water systems on reserves across Canada. Engineers have expressed scepticism that the goal of eliminating all boil-water advisories by 2021 can be met, and the entire history of Ottawa's relations with First Nations suggests scepticism.

Ensuring that reserves have pure water does not necessarily end the problem, however. The Garden Hill Reserve 600 km northeast of Winnipeg has a proper clean water facility, but half the homes are not connected to it, 180 of them because they are unsafe to live in. They are to be provided with clean water by truck, but there are not enough trucks so water is stored in cisterns half of which the reserve could not afford to clean in 2018, 30% of which did not meet national safety standards. Garden Hill Reserve is not a priority because it is not under an advisory, but Ottawa is studying the problem.

What is clear in 2019 is that no previous government has made as firm a commitment or followed it up as strongly. Eighty-seven advisories have been lifted, 52 more than in the previous 3 ½ years. Thirty-nine new ones were added, and the total number in effect dropped from 105 in 2015 to 56 on July 31, 2019. Even if all houses on all reserves had clean drinking water by 2021 and new problems were dealt with quickly and properly, the legacy of the past will not soon disappear. Generations of First Nations have grown up and lived for decades in conditions that would never have been tolerated in Canadian municipalities. Their pleas for something as simple as clean drinking water went unheard and unaddressed by a succession of Conservative and Liberal federal governments. In April 2019 58 advisories were still in effect, but more might be added as other contaminants in the water are identified as health risks.

There is an inexplicable paradox in federal underfunding of water infrastructure on the reserves. Beginning in the 1960s, the federal government launched more and more infrastructure programs in Canadian municipalities. It has no responsibility for such infrastructure and, indeed, its programs were a violation of the constitution which gives exclusive responsibility for municipalities to the provinces. Ottawa often dictated the terms and used its "spending power" to force provinces and municipalities to pay a large portion of the costs - if they did not accept the federal plan with its conditions, taxes collected in those municipalities would be spent elsewhere.

For decades provinces objected to this encroachment on their responsibility and the resulting distortions to their budgets and priorities, and this federal interference was one of the major factors behind support for Quebec separatism. Ottawa also spent Canadian tax dollars abroad on water projects. Yet the same government at the same time was ignoring its own clear constitutional and ethical responsibilities, allowing hundreds of thousands of citizens to live in Third World conditions. Though the gap is closing, the Third World conditions continue today. Ignorance helps explain it: an Angus Reid poll of June 7, 2018, indicated that one-third of Canadians believed that Ottawa spends too much on Indigenous issues!

Chapter 14

Education, Health, and Housing

At the time of contact with Europeans, First Nations had their own systems of education, health, and welfare and lived in housing that was suitable for the environment, their nomadic lifestyle, and the resources available. These factors were vastly different from those in Europe, but they were effective. As in Europe, these systems varied greatly across the continent, but as in Europe, there were many commonalities. Villages had medicine men who administered a wide range of herbal remedies plus what might be called psychological remedies including dances, prayers, and smoke houses, and First Nations throughout the Americas were relatively healthy before the introduction of European diseases.

In terms of what is now called welfare, society was organized communally and food was divided amongst all the villagers. The old, injured and ill were looked after by the healthy. A major responsibility of chiefs was to ensure that food was distributed and when there was starvation, which was often in many areas, everyone went hungry.

In the twenty-first century the picture is vastly different. Indigenous children are below average by every indicator: family income, access to clean water, infant mortality, crowding, and homelessness. The average child poverty rate in Canada is 17%, for Indigenous people it is 40%, for those Indigenous who are First Nations it is over 50%. A 2019 study prepared for the AFN indicated that the poverty rate of First Nations children was 47%, unchanged over the previous decade. A 1995 report stated that infant mortality was well above national levels and death from violence was three times the national average. Their rate of diabetes is three times the average, their suicide rate 5-7 time the average.

A 1985 report said half of reserve housing failed to meet basic standards, one third was seriously overcrowded and that people were five times as likely to live in crowded housing and three times as likely to live in house requiring repairs as non-Indigenous people. Thirty percent of non-Indigenous Canadians have a university degree, for Indigenous

Canadians the figure is 10%. There are problems with these statistics, and the 2018 Auditor General's Report sharply criticized Ottawa for not collecting accurate data on social indicators on reserves. One example was that the number of students graduating from high school was half what Ottawa reported. Clearly something went very wrong between 1600 and 2000 and it is still very wrong.

In 1600 the First Nations systems of education were hardly formalized, but they were very effective in the one thing that mattered - results. By the time boys and girls reached maturity, they knew how to do the jobs expected of them such as hunting, cooking, or making clothing and how to function as spouses and parents and look after elders. They understood how their communities functioned, decision-making, the selection and role of leaders and medicine men, the need for discipline on hunting or war parties, and they knew their culture, history, and traditions.

Their ability to memorize what was agreed in oral negotiations and to pass that information to future generations was a continuous thorn in the side of European and later Canadian governments which often left key oral promises out of written texts. This successful system of education was achieved without formal classes, textbooks, teachers, the tyranny of the clock, or physical discipline - the first time Indigenous children encountered physical discipline was in white schools. Interestingly, in the last 50 years, Canadian schools have abandoned the strap and adopted the traditions First Nations had used for centuries.

After contact, Europeans and later Canadians gradually added a layer of their systems of education, health and welfare to the First Nations ones. Missionaries entered the villages and began teaching Christianity and European ways and providing medical services. Governments began providing assistance. Schools and hospitals were established. When treaties were negotiated, these European and Canadian government services were formalized and documented, but they were still an addition to First Nations forms of education, health and welfare.

The best indication of federal government responsibilities towards First Nations in terms of education, health and welfare are the treaties that were negotiated on the prairies. Each was slightly different but in general they came to represent Ottawa's overall commitment to all First Nations across the country. In these treaties, First Nations surrendered their lands in return for several federal commitments including ones covering education, health and welfare. It was accepted by both sides that the First Nations were transitioning from their previous economy based on hunting to the Canadian one based on agriculture, and Ottawa was going to help them make that transition and provide for them as they made the leap.

The Commissioners made this very clear in the speeches they gave at the beginnings of the negotiations. Commissioner Adams Archibald opened the 1871 negotiations saying the Queen wished them to be "happy and content" and "to make them free of famine and distress," to "make their homes more comfortable," and to "live and prosper." At the negotiations for Treaty 4, Commissioner Alexander Morris said that the Queen would "protect their way of life." They were promised relief from "calamities and famine," and relief in case of actual destitution, that is, welfare.

The promise in Treaty 6 for help with "pestilence and famine" was repeated in subsequent treaties. Most of the treaties called for a "medicine chest" in each agent's house, that is, if someone was ill, he could go to the agent for free medicine. At the negotiations for Treaty 8, an oral promise was made for supplies of medicine. Most of the treaties addressed one of the main health concerns by prohibiting liquor on the reserves. A 1935 Supreme Court decision (Dreaver v. King) confirmed that Ottawa was responsible for health services for First Nations.

The education rights were much more specific. Commissioner Archibald set the tone, saying education created a "future of promise." First Nations "will be as well able to take care of themselves as the whites around them." There was to be a school on each reserve when they requested it. This was not an extraordinary offer because Ottawa set aside two sections of land in every township of 36 sections to support education for white settlers. The latter then build one-room schoolhouses roughly four or five miles apart, an easy horse-back ride from the surrounding farms. The treaties did not transfer control of education from First Nations to Ottawa. Ottawa would build schools and provide teachers who would prepare students for the new world they were entering, but the schools would be an addition to their culture and be under their control just as the nearby schools were under the control of local school boards. Education was thus a fundamental part of the new partnership.

These promises, both written and oral, were broken almost immediately by the federal government. Regarding education, Ottawa did not build a school on each reserve, it did not leave First Nations in control of education, and it regarded the new Canadian education as a replacement rather than an addition to First Nations culture. Instead, it established residential schools, took perhaps half the children from their homes, and left half on the reserves without proper education assistance.

Inasmuch as Ottawa did attempt to meet its obligations for Indigenous education, the funding was always woefully inadequate. In 1941, it was estimated that Ottawa was spending $41 per student compared to $58 by the provinces. In 2009, a Parliamentary Budget Office (PBO) report said the federal schools were systematically underfunded by 58%. In December 2016, the PBO said that the shortfall in federal spending compared to the provinces was $600M. In Ontario, Ottawa was spending $14,500 per student on reserve schools but the figure would have been $21-25,000 using the provincial formula for calculating costs.

Another estimate suggested that Ottawa paid a reserve in Ontario $8,000 per year per student but paid the Ontario government $16,000 if a Status Indian was enrolled in a provincial school. Status Indians have the right to funding for university but between 2001 and 2006, 10,000 qualified students could not get this funding. The 1997 budget capped the growth in DIA's budget at 2% annually which led to an 18% decline in the number of university students funded over the next decade while the number graduating from high school was increasing. A 2015 DIA report said spending should be increased from 2% to 4.5% annually. It wasn't. It should not have been a surprise when, in 2011, a school in Manitoba was closed because it had been overrun with snakes.

The result of this was entirely predictable: 25% of low income non-Indigenous Canadians do not have high school education, for First Nations the figure is 60%. Thirty percent of non-Indigenous Canadians have a university degree, for Indigenous Canadians the figure is 10%. In Saskatchewan in 2017, the high school graduation rate was 85% for non-Indigenous students compared to 43% for Indigenous ones. The low level of education then feeds into the vicious circle of poor health, unemployment, poverty, housing, alcohol and drug abuse, and high incarceration rates.

In the 2015 election, the federal Liberals promised to deal with the gap in spending on education – at the time reserve schools were receiving $3,500 less per student than provincial ones and were the only ones that did not have a fixed funding base. The 2016 budget promised $2.6B over four years plus $500M over three years for infrastructure. As with most budgets, the figures were fudged, and the fine print indicated that this amount was spread over five years with $800M in the 5th year. That would be after the government's mandate expired, subject to change by a new government, and meant that the actual amount promised by the Trudeau government during its mandate was $1.8B not $2.6B with the smallest investment coming in the first two years.

In September 2018, First Nations leaders said that the money promised in 2016 had not yet arrived. Chief Peter Beatty of the Peter Ballantyne band said there had been no increase in core funding and that funding had only arrived for projects that had to be applied for every year. Ottawa was still targeting the money, spending much less than the provinces, and making the decisions.

Meanwhile a significant change was taking place in the structure of education. The residential schools were a failure from the beginning and after over 120 years of failure the government decided to make changes. In the 1960s, it began closing the residential schools, building more schools on reserves, and sending more Status Indians to provincial schools. Both reserve and provincial schools provided far better education and the gap between First Nations and non-Indigenous graduates began to narrow. Sending Status Indians to provincial schools was another form of assimilation, though, and the Indian Brotherhood called for First Nations control of their own education. In the 1970s, Ottawa responded so there are more schools on reserves, more First Nations teachers, more relevant curricula, more Indigenous language instruction and culture courses, and the schools and their graduates are far more successful.

The number of schools on reserves increased from 53 in 1975 to 353 in 1992. Most bands now administer their schools and teach the provincial curricula plus language and culture. By 1992, 50% of students were in band-operated schools, 45% in provincial schools, only 5% in federal ones. In 1960, only 3% of students got to grade 12, by 1992 it was 60%. In 1992, the number of Indigenous students in university was

22,000, doubled from 1985. Numerous universities have Indigenous programs, schools are introducing more of them, more and better information is available, and more balanced history is being written and taught. Canada now has over 500 reserve schools with 110,000 students but many are in remote areas and have special needs.

But funding is still woefully inadequate - on August 31, 2018, Kashechewan First Nations closed its portable classrooms just before school re-opening because they were unfit to use. Oddly, Ottawa still fails to spend all the money budgeted. Progress continues to be made on restructuring the system. After two years of negotiations, agreement was announced on January 24, 2019, to re-allocate the annual $1.9B education budget. More will go to core funding which is stable instead of program funding which is decided on a case-by-case basis. That also gives bands greater control over education. As part of its commitment to preserving Indigenous culture, schools would receive $1,500 per student to promote language and culture.

The situation is similar with health services where some specific examples will paint as good (or bad) a picture as the statistics do for education. Indigenous Canadians are entitled to dental service but are not getting it and the incidence of dental disease is twice the national average. Because there are too few dentists, they tend to concentrate on emergency work. DIA's response to complaints is to quote the allegedly large amounts in budgets. As with other problems with Indigenous peoples, DIA seems to be more willing to spend money fighting court cases than delivering services for which it is responsible.

From 2010 to 2015 the DIA was one of the highest spending departments for legal fees, spending approximately half a billion dollars a year. In 2017, it spent $110,000 fighting a claim by Josey Willier, a Cree from Calgary, for $6,000 for dental work that two dentists said was necessary. They had seen Willier; Health Canada consulted four dentists who had not. Attention has repeatedly been focussed on the amount of money Ottawa spends fighting claims for services. Provincial health care systems have better data and targets making it difficult to compare federal spending to service for non-Indigenous Canadians.

The federal government has not responded to this situation with a comprehensive policy. Instead announcements are doled out like other federal press releases and photo-ops. In 2016, the government announced the spending of $382M over 3 years for First Nations children who had disabilities. That was good but left unanswered what it was doing for those children who did not have disabilities plus all the adults. On September 6, 2018, Minister Philpott announced the spending of $68M over 3 years for dozens of First Nations communities in the three prairie provinces with details still to be worked out. First Nations and others might ask: What about the other seven provinces? What happens in three years? Who decides the details? How long does it take to fix health at this rate? How many headlines can be squeezed out of the budget at $68M per photo-op?

One of the saddest examples of dysfunctional federalism was the death of a First Nations child in 2005 while the federal and Manitoba governments squabbled over who should pay his medical expenses. His name was Jordan Rivers Anderson and the outcome was a Parliamentary Motion (296) of December 2007, stating that when services are needed, they must be provided immediately by the first level of government that is aware of the need, and any debate over payment must take place later. It became known as Jordan's Principle. Despite the Motion, the government continued to fight against paying for emergency health services on reserves. On April 27, 2010, the Human Rights Tribunal confirmed the Commons Motion and on May 10 the government said it was accepting it and there was to be no delay in providing services due to disputes between Ottawa and the provinces or between federal departments.

But in August 2014, the Caring Society and Amnesty International went to the Canadian Human Rights Tribunal arguing that the government was not applying Jordan's Principle as Parliament intended. In December 2016, the Tribunal ruled that Ottawa had to close the gap "immediately" between the amount it was spending on child welfare and the amount the provinces were spending, a ruling directly related to health because the shortage in spending on health especially for mental health and special needs was one of the reasons children needed welfare.

Documents revealed that Health Canada officials were well aware of the gap but had no plans to close it and were left scrambling by the order to do so "immediately." That gave credence to the charge that without the Tribunal's order they would not have acted to close the gap and that the Department knew that underfunding health was forcing families to put their children in welfare. In 2016, the Department of Health still had no agreed definition of Jordan's Principle which had been adopted in 2007 and finally in May 2017, it accepted the definition in the Human Rights Tribunal ruling. The current government has substantially increased funding for Indigenous health and welfare, but it has also continued fighting to avoid paying for some individual cases.

The new government's 2016 budget allocated $127M for Jordan's Principle cases, and Ministers Bennett and Philpott said the budget was proof that the government was complying with the Human Rights Tribunal. NDP MP Charlie Angus said their comment was "disingenuous." In fact, eight months later Health Canada had spent only $11.4M on 1,500 children. Health Canada said that it had difficulty identifying cases, and by February 2017, it had helped 20 in Atlantic Canada, 600 in Ontario, 400 in Saskatchewan, and over 2,200 in Manitoba, an inexplicable discrepancy in numbers. Charlie Angus also pointed out that only 22 children had received help in Ontario in the previous six months when there were 26 high-risk children on the Wapekeka reserve in his constituency alone. But the current budget claims that 214,000 cases have been approved since July 2016. On November 15, 2018, Alberta became the first province to accept fully its responsibilities under Jordan's Principle when it signed an agreement with the federal government and 11 First Nations.

In January 2019, Jordan's Principle was back before the Human Rights Tribunal, and the plaintiff once more was Cindy Blackstock of the First Nations Child and Family Caring Society. In this case, Ottawa had refused funding for medical treatment for a non-Status child whose mother and grandmother had Status. The argument was that the Tribunal's original ruling had not distinguished between Status and non-status Indians. On February 21 the Tribunal ruled that non-status First Nations were to be covered until the definition of First Nations was resolved, a process that is ongoing. The 2019 budget continued funding for Jordan's Principle at $1.5B but with no provision for inflation or population growth.

There is also a "residential school" aspect to health care. Between 1945 and 1981, 29 Indigenous hospitals were operated in Canada. Like residential schools, they were underfunded, overcrowded, and improperly staffed compared to facilities available to non-Indigenous Canadians (racial discrimination). Some were in former army barracks, some in segregated annexes of regular hospitals. Experiments were done on patients and the death rate from tuberculosis was amongst the highest ever recorded. As in the residential schools, children were shackled to their beds. Complaints of sexual and physical abuse have emerged, and survivors launched a $1.1B class-action lawsuit on January 25, 2018.

Few things symbolize the problems of health, resource development and relations between First Nations and the government as much as the words "Grassy Narrows." In the 1960s and 70s the Reed Paper company released 9,000 Kg of mercury contaminated effluent into the English-Wabigoon river near the First Nations reserve of Grassy Narrows northeast of Kenora, Ontario. The mercury destroyed a successful fishing industry and had devastating effects on the health of the residents. They are six times as likely to have health problems as other First Nations, and 90% of them suffer from some form of mercury poisoning which is passed from mother to child.

For half a century government action fell far short of what was needed. The current plan is to build a $90M medical facility. All the negotiations have been completed except for one problem: Chief Rudy Turtle does not trust the government when it says that the agreement guarantees funding for 30 years. He wants the money put in a trust fund now so that no future government can reduce or eliminate it. That, apparently, is what the provincial government did with the $85M it provided to clean up the river. Ottawa argues that the wording is adequate, so the agreement has not been signed and a frustrated Chief Turtle has decided to run for the NDP in the October federal election.

None of this is surprising. Since at least the mid-1960s the federal government has attempted to pass responsibility and costs for Indigenous health to the provinces. The provinces were infuriated because at the same time, Ottawa was initiating Medicare for non-Indigenous Canadians, a federal program within provincial jurisdiction in which the provinces would have to pay half the costs according to criteria established by Ottawa. Medicare was a marvelous program and became a Canadian "value," but at the time it was initiated, Ottawa was dismally failing its own responsibilities for the Canadians for whom it was solely responsible – Indigenous ones. At that time life expectancy for the average Canadian man was 79, for Indigenous ones it was 74; for the average Canadian women it was 83, for Indigenous ones it was 80. The infant mortality rate for Indigenous Canadians was two to four times the average, the stroke rate two times the average. Medicare was directed towards the wrong Canadians.

Housing is another area of crisis. A 1985 report said that half of reserve housing failed to meet basic standards, one third was seriously overcrowded and that people were five times as likely to live in crowded housing and three times as likely to live in houses requiring repairs as non-Indigenous Canadians. Poor housing affected all other indicators – health, education, suicide, drug abuse, and violence. In 2011, a DIA report indicated that 20-30,000 houses were needed, 16,900 needed repair and another 5,200 needed replacing, but the AFN put the figure for new houses needed at 85,000.

There were as many as 18 people per house, 40%-50% of which needed major repairs. The DIA housing budget was around $270M but the AFN said that around $450M was needed. First Nations are 10 times as likely to die in house fires as other Canadians, a figure that speaks to housing, water supply, infrastructure, poverty, education, and the undermining of band governments.

Public attention was aroused when the crisis in the community of Attawapiskat in northern Ontario made the national news, with people living in sheds and tents in freezing weather. Five years later a DIA report said Manitoba had the worst First Nations housing in Canada and that it would cost $2B to fix, 13 times the whole DIA housing budget of $150M, and that the situation was deteriorating. Statistics from the Quebec Cree Nation Government indicated a backlog of 3,000 houses which was projected to grow to 4,500 at current rates. In December 2018, its executive director Bill Namagoose pointed out that the situation would produce migration to the cities. Underfunding of housing on reserves thus continues the federal policy of assimilation by driving First Nations into overwhelmingly non-Indigenous urban environments.

A CBC report of February 6 said that of 17,289 houses in Manitoba, 4,176 needed major repairs and 1,212 needed replacement. The article suggests that Ottawa still controls construction and repair house-by-house and the reserves lack resources for proper maintenance. A new crisis hit the news in February 2019 on the Cat Lake reserve 400 km north of Thunder Bay. A month earlier the council had declared a state of emergency arguing that three quarters of the houses had to be replaced due to mould, a problem due to building housing with ventilation and insulation that is inappropriate for the northern climate. After three medical evacuations, it declared a state of emergency and invoked Jordan's Principle to force action.

The publicity brought verbal and political results, the announcement of an interim agreement on February 21 of $12.8M for repairs and new houses. That created yet another scandal, because in 2017 the band had hired a consultant to help obtain more funding from Ottawa, and his contract provided for 10% of any resulting funds. He is now claiming $1.28M but Chief Matthew Keewaykapow says he was not involved in the recent negotiations with Ottawa. The situation on Cat Lake was well know and little different from that on other northern reserves, so apart from helping shine the spotlight on a particular reserve, it is not clear how consultants help the overall situation, and the money to be spent on Cat Lake may simply be transferred from other reserves or budgets or not spent once attention shifts elsewhere.

Some reports say the problem is that people on reserves cannot own their houses and cannot therefore obtain mortgages and loans to repair them, but much of the housing is adequate and some reserves have found ways for people to own their houses. This is an excuse - non-Indigenous rental housing does not suffer the same level of neglect as reserve housing; and the reserve landlord is the government. In *The Unjust Society*, Harold Cardinal gave an example of the problems with housing. Houses were built on one reserve but soon the foundations shifted, the doors and windows would not close properly and the project was a disaster. An official 800 km away had decided on the location and he put it in a swamp. The 2016 budget doubled spending on housing, but AFN Regional Chief Kevin Hart said it would take generations to overcome the backlog.

In November 2017, Ottawa announced a long-awaited National Housing Strategy but said that more consultations were required before developing a promised Indigenous Housing Strategy. By that time, Indigenous people living off reserve were ten times as likely to be homeless as non-Indigenous Canadians. The 2017 budget had provided $25 million for off-reserve housing for the whole of Canada over 10 years. The 2018 budget promised $600M over three years and on February 20, 2019, Ottawa announced that it would spend $638M on urban housing for Indigenous people as part of the overall housing strategy to address homelessness. That was criticized since it did not address the other urban housing issues. Indigenous housing was falling further behind because Ottawa had its priorities backwards, dealing first with the group who needed help the least but had the most votes. The main problem, in short, was and remains massive underfunding, the same problem as for education, health, social services, and other forms of infrastructure such as clean water.

Chapter 15

Consultations: why bother? Well...

In the long relationship between First Nations and the Canadian government, the latter's attitude towards meaningful consultations seems to have been that they are not needed, not "as long as the sun shines and the rivers flow." There has never been a time when Ottawa demonstrated that it believed the views of First Nations had to be solicited and then taken into account in the development of policies and the making of decisions that affected those nations.

In 2016, the Federal Court of Appeal rejected the government's approval of the proposed Enbridge Northern Gateway pipeline partly because First Nations along the route had not been properly consulted. On August 30, 2018, the same Court rejected the approval for the Kinder-Morgan Trans Mountain pipeline for the exact same reason. The Trudeau government made a much better attempt in 2019 but as of September 2019 it too is headed back to the courts.

The failure to consult has a long, unfortunate and costly history because decisions that are made without input from those affected are rarely the best and are often the worst. They may also be unstable, uncertain and impermanent because those not consulted or their children, grandchildren or great-grandchildren may take action to reverse decisions. First Nations have always reacted negatively to failure to consult. In 1875 the Cree blocked the construction of a telegraph line because no one asked them for permission to cross their land. When the prairie provinces were created, Ottawa retained control of land. When that control was transferred to the provincial governments in 1930, First Nations were not consulted even though the transfer had serious implications for them especially regarding rights for hunting and fishing. That remains a problem to this day.

One of the early acts of the new central government was passing the Indian Act of 1876 with the goal of assimilating First Nations into Canadian society. They were not consulted on the drafting of the most crucial piece of legislation affecting them, on most of the amendments and legislation that fleshed out or changed the Indian Act, or on the policy for the residential schools. Failure to consult remained the history of "consultations" for over a century. As the conditions of First Nations deteriorated, the federal government appointed several commissions to study the situation and make recommendations. First Nations were sometimes consulted but their views or the recommendations were usually ignored. There were no consultations when crucial decisions were made in 1966 to share federal and provincial services in welfare, a decision that led to decades of confusion, underfunding and buck-passing that the current government is trying to sort out in the last months of its mandate.

One of the worst examples regarding "consultations" was the development of the government's White Paper in 1969. Prime Minister Pierre Trudeau had major plans to introduce his concepts of a "Just Society," which centered on equal rights for all Canadians. Trudeau did not accept that First Nations were a separate race from other Canadians, that Canada should have treaties with its own people, or that Canada owed them compensation for previous injustices. The constitutional changes he wanted required abolishing the Indian Act. In preparation for that his Minister of Indian Affairs, Jean Chrétien, was dispatched across the country for an extensive round of consultations with First Nations who eagerly responded to the invitation to provide inputs into the policy review.

The White Paper that was tabled in Parliament on June 25, 1969, came as a bitter shock. It did not contain the recommendations First Nations had spent so much time refining and promoting. Instead, it was a blueprint to go in the opposite direction, to finalize Macdonald's policy of assimilation. It acknowledged problems like poverty and high incarceration rates but incorrectly blamed them on separate status and said the problems would disappear if First Nations were assimilated, the old goal of the Indian Act. If enacted, First Nations would lose their rights and they, their reserves, and federal programs would "disappear." There was outrage at the betrayal and with the government's false claim that the document was based on "consultations." Outrage mounted and the government was forced to abandon the White Paper, at least as official policy.

Two of PM Pierre Trudeau's top priorities were entrenching a Charter of Rights in the Canadian Constitution and then patriating it from Great Britain. Trudeau was determined to obtain the agreement of the provinces for a Charter and an amending formula and he launched a series of meetings with provincial premiers but did not include First Nations leaders. Trudeau did not understand that the British connection to the Canadian constitution was extremely important to First Nations.

Their treaties were with the British Crown and had been negotiated by lieutenant governors and commissioners on behalf of British Queens and Kings. While Britain had recognized Canadian sovereignty in 1931, First Nations had never surrendered sovereignty to Britain, and as far as they were concerned, they still had a special relationship with the British Crown and the British government still had a responsibility to them. Patriation would sever the link they still believed they had with an important institution and country that could protect them to some degree from the white man's government in Ottawa.

For First Nations, patriation of the BNA Act was a matter for Ottawa, the provinces, and them, and they had every right to be "meaningfully consulted" and to be partners in the process. In 1979, they began lobbying British politicians and opinion-makers arguing that the BNA Act could not be patriated without their consent and that their rights had to be entrenched in it before patriation. While Trudeau and others thought the British government would rubber stamp any proposal sent to them, First Nations leaders and others convinced many in Britain that the Crown, in this case the British government, had an outstanding obligation to them that had not been surrendered in 1931. If not, why was the British government debating the Canadian constitution and preparing to pass a law in London containing changes of fundamental importance to Canadians?

This lobbying combined with that of other opponents of Trudeau's goals and methods paid off. He was forced to go back to the drawing board with the premiers. First Nations were excluded from the meetings of 1980-82 when the first ministers worked out their agreements on the Charter and patriation, but a new Section 35 recognizing Aboriginal rights was added to the Constitution. The rights were not specified - that was to be done in several rounds of negotiations. An important precedent had been established - Ottawa could no longer impose its views without holding consultations. Negotiations took place in 1983, 1984, 1985, and 1987 but no agreement emerged on what specific rights were protected by the new Charter. Defining the rights guaranteed in Section 35 was left to the courts,

In the view of some Canadians, Trudeau's Charter, the patriation and the way it was done had several defects and in 1984 the new Prime Minister, Brian Mulroney, set out to fix them. After the failure of the meetings designed to define Aboriginal rights, he and the premiers turned to dealing with Quebec's demands. They did so without the participation of First Nations and the latter were infuriated both at being left out and at the speed with which Quebec's concerns could be agreed upon – one day - while theirs remained unaddressed. Mulroney's Meech Lake Accord came to grief three years later when Elijah Harper, a Cree MLA in the Manitoba Legislature, refused unanimous consent to a motion to extend the debate allowing Meech to die of exhaustion.

Both Liberal and Conservative politicians were beginning to learn that failure to consult First Nations on constitutional issues that affected them could carry very serious consequences. When Mulroney attempted once more to fix the Constitution, this time with the Charlottetown Accord, First Nations leaders were for the first time included in the talks. Some of their demands were incorporated in that agreement but it failed to be ratified, partly because the Indian Act had effectively excluded First Nations women from leadership and hence a role in the negotiations and many of them voted against it. Since then, First Nations leaders have been invited to heads-of-government meetings. That now includes the annual conference of premiers.

Actions by the Harper government led to another refinement of the question of consultations. In 2012, it introduced an omnibus tax bill, C-45, which affected the hunting and fishing rights of, amongst others, the Mikisew Cree band in Alberta. There were no consultations with them, and they argued that the bill interfered with rights provided in Treaty 8, which might now be guaranteed by Section 35 of the 1982 Constitution. They launched a court case arguing that they had the right to be consulted on the development of such legislation. On September 11, 2018, the Supreme Court rejected the case by a 7:2 vote, arguing that the courts cannot become involved in legislation at the drafting stage.

The Court did, however, confirm that Parliament had an obligation to act "honourably" when developing legislation that affects First Nations.

Harper's attempt to use the omnibus bill to sneak through reductions to First Nations rights also produced possibly the biggest civil rights movement in Canadian history. In November 2012, four First Nations women in Saskatchewan held a teach-in to disseminate information and criticism of the Bill. That initiative was rapidly reproduced elsewhere, and social media created a snow-ball effect across Canada that became known as the Idle No More movement.

It was really the "Not Silent This Time" movement as First Nations had hardly been idle, but the message was that they could not remain "idle" regarding this particular law. Soon there were hundreds of demonstrations in shopping malls and on city streets accompanied by blockades of roads, railways and bridges. Chief Theresa Spence of the Attawapiskat First Nation joined in with a well-publicized hunger strike in Ottawa protesting conditions on her reserve.

The movement was largely spontaneous, female-driven, leaderless, and supported by many non-Indigenous Canadians. It received extensive media coverage and support around the world. The list of demands gradually expanded to include defending land, treaties and rights, having an inquiry into missing and murdered women, better education and housing, acceptance of the UN Declaration of the Rights of Indigenous Peoples, and other issues.

It was a criticism of federal policies but also of the failure of the AFN and band leaders and of what was perceived by many to be an overly cozy relationship between many of those leaders and the government. It was also an assertion of female power and thus a threat to the male-dominated governance Ottawa had imposed on the bands through the Indian Act. AFN leaders and Chief Spence demanded a meeting with the Crown, in this case meaning both PM Harper and Governor General David Johnston.

After acrimonious negotiations, Harper met some Chiefs on January 11, 2013 while other Chiefs refused to attend. Little was agreed, Spence abandoned her controversial hunger strike, and Idle No More eventually petered out. The legacy was important, however. Out of nowhere, failure to consult had produced an enormous, spontaneous, female-led, cross-Canada movement which carried the potential to do serious damage to the economy. While public opinion did not support it, there was no question that awareness and sympathy had increased. Those who participated had found a new sense of power and purpose, and the importance and unpredictability of social media had emerged from the shadows. Two years later many of the demands of Idle No More were in the platform of the Liberal Party of Canada; Canada was heading for an election; and First Nations participation would reach a high level and have an impact.

Failure to consult is not just a problem for resource development in the West and North. In Nova Scotia the Mi'kmaq objected to a plan by Alton Gas to store natural gas in underground caves hear the Shubenacadie River. The province argued in 2016 that it had no obligation to consult because the Mi'kmaq were a conquered people, which was not true. Then Premier Stephen McNeil apologized and said that was not the government's position. The lawyer who handled the province's case sued the government and demanded that his instructions from the province be released. The province tried to keep them secret. On July 4, 2019, a court ordered the government to release the instructions so the public will obtain a glimpse of Nova Scotia's official position on consultations with First Nations.

Building pipelines has become the major flashpoint in terms of consultations. The background was that some important court cases had ended the century-old practice of developing resource projects without consulting affected First Nations. A key case was the 2004 Supreme Court decision on mining and logging proposals that ordered the government to consult and make appropriate efforts to accommodate the concerns that had been raised before approving such projects (Haida Nation v. British Columbia). These court decisions did not give First Nations a veto over the projects: if concerns raised by First Nations were deemed to be valid, they had to be addressed, if not, they could be ignored. But it is the courts that make the decision, not First Nations, governments, or regulatory agencies.

One of the major oil pipeline projects that ran into serious problems over consultations was the Enbridge Northern Gateway line from Alberta to the Kitimat on the Pacific. The National Energy Board (NEB) approved it with 208 conditions after which Ottawa was to hold consultations with First Nations and perhaps attach more conditions. Unlike the NEB hearings with non-Indigenous Canadians, the Harper government rubber-stamped the project with no additional conditions and in 2016 the Federal Court of Appeal overturned that decision by a 3:2 vote on the grounds that the consultations with First Nations had been "brief, hurried and inadequate." In effect, the NEB's "consultations" with non-Indigenous Canadians had been done properly; the governments "consultations" with First Nations had been a farce. The new Trudeau government had the option of proceeding with the pipeline after carrying out a new round of "meaningful consultations" but it dropped the project.

At the same time the Kinder Morgan company was working on its plan to add a third pipeline to its existing Trans Mountain line from Alberta to Burnaby, the TMX, a project that did have the new Trudeau government's blessing. In May 2016, after hearings (or consultatns) with non-Indigenous Canadians, the NEB approved it with 157 conditions. The new Liberal government confirmed that decision in November 2016 but was obliged to consult First Nations along the route and possibly add more conditions. This it promised to do in a far more meaningful way than Harper had done with Northern Gateway. In subsequent months First Nations and others found problems with the project and 18 legal cases were launched against it.

On August 30, 2018, the Federal Court of Appeal combined all the cases against Trans Mountain into one and rejected the Trudeau government's approval of it by a 3:0 vote. That was a more definitive rejection than that of Northern Gateway and was made under the same judge. The Court found that the government had not properly consulted First Nations and had not dealt with the fact that the NEB had incorrectly excluded consideration of the possible effects of tanker traffic on the marine environment, something of great concern to coastal First Nations. In effect, the government approved the pipeline before beginning consultations, repeatedly said it would be built, and listened to concerns and passed them on to the NEB without indicating any action that should be taken to meet the concerns. There was no ambiguity in the Court's ruling as it used the word "failure" over 100 times in the 272-page document.

Ottawa had provided "process," which was an improvement on Harper's by being more "lengthy," but it had not provided "substance" in the form of identifying responses to the concerns that were raised, that is, rejecting them with reasons or adding new conditions. As First Nations spokesmen said, it had just ticked off a box "consultations done." The Court ordered the government to do the consultations in a meaningful way just as it had previously ordered for Northern Gateway. After the court decision Minister Bennett said: "It means we will actually have to design a process (of consultations) that's better," in effect repeating what Trudeau had said two years earlier and confirming that the Trudeau government still did not have a proper process of consultations. Two days after Trans Mountain was rejected, CBC carried the following headline: "Quebec offers $3.1M for Kahnawake land grievance without consulting community" indicating that it is not only Ottawa that has a problem with consultations.

So much uncertainty had been created that Kinder Morgan appeared to lose interest so in May 2018, the government bought the existing pipeline for $4.5B. That seemed to guarantee that the addition would be built which again called into question how meaningful consultations would be if First Nations raised objections that could not be accommodated. Alternately, it suggested that objections had to be accommodated, that is, that by purchasing the pipeline and stating that the additional one would be built, the government had put itself in a position in which any and all First Nations concerns had to be accommodated.

The government gave the NEB a new deadline to consider the tanker traffic issue. That process began in Calgary on November 20 when the first of 45 Indigenous groups met the NEB panel. On February 22 the NEB approved the project again, confirming 156 of the original 157 conditions and adding 16 non-binding recommendations to deal with marine environment issues. It acknowledged the dangers to the environment but said they were outweighed by the advantages to the economy. Indigenous leaders and environmentalists immediately condemned the report. The new round of "meaningful consultations" with 129 First Nations was headed by retired justice Frank Iacobucci. According to Minister of Natural Resources Amarjeet Sohi, the number of people doing the consultations was doubled to 60 and given proper training and a proper mandate, suggesting that had not been done two years earlier. Sohi himself held 48 meetings with 65 Indigenous groups.

On Tuesday, June 18, PM Trudeau announced that the government had approved the extension and that construction would proceed within months. It had accepted the NEB's second approval with its 16 new non-binding recommendations for dealing with tanker traffic. Regarding consultations with First Nations, Ottawa had, in its own opinion, carried out "meaningful consultations" according to the conditions laid down by the Court of Appeal. The government was, Trudeau said, "responding meaningfully to the concerns they have wherever possible," and the consultations resulted in "changes …to the NEB conditions…" "We listened, and we are acting on what we heard." Minister Sohi added: "We are satisfied that we have discharged our duty to consult with Indigenous communities."

This decision was based on the 233-page Crown Consultation and Accommodation Report which documents the second consultation process with First Nations, who was consulted, when and how, what advice was sought, the number of meetings, and the engagement of ministers and senior officials. Accordingly, after listening to every expression of concern ("meaningful consultations"), officials drew up a list of government responses ("accommodation"). That was distributed to First Nations with adequate time to comment. It was re-drafted and is the core of the Report (pp. 144-190). That chapter documents changes to the route, measures such as burying the pipeline deeper or using thicker pipe, measures to deal with oil spills, and other means of meeting concerns.

The Report is a mixture of the new measures or conditions TMX and the government must meet, the things that were already being done, things left for future negotiations, and a laundry list of all the things Ottawa does for First Nations everywhere which could mitigate the problems caused by the pipeline, with a liberal sprinkling of words like "may" and "wherever possible" plus other qualifiers and things that might be done in the future. It is, in short, a typically confusing bureaucratic document, possibly deliberately so. Forty-four bands or nations have signed commercial agreements worth $400M covering compensation, payments, and employment opportunities but in signing on they had to agree that consultations had been adequate, that the project has their consent, and that they will not obstruct it.

Several First Nations immediately rejected the government's assertion that this second attempt at consultations had been adequate and meaningful, including the Squamish, Coldwater, Sema:th, and

Tsleil-Waututh Nations. They pointed out that the government had already made up its mind before the consultations began. Some argue that the government does not have their consent to proceed, but the Supreme Court has not said that "meaningful consultations" includes the right of veto.

The United Nations Declaration on the Rights of Indigenous Peoples seems to imply a right of veto, but while the Liberal Party endorsed that Declaration, a private members Bill to enforce it did not pass Parliament. The Liberals had not made it government policy but have included it in their 1919 election platform, so it is still not quite clear where they stand on First Nations right of veto or consent. Bill C-69 does not seem to make it clear either and will likely require further court cases to determine the line between "meaningful consultations," veto, and consent. In the drafting of that legislation, First Nations leaders who support energy development such as Roy Fox, Chief of the Kainai Blood Tribe, said that in its consultations the government listened to the First Nations that agreed with the proposed legislation, not the ones that had concerns with it.

Grand Chief Stewart Phillip of the Union of BC Indian Chiefs was one of several to predict renewed resistance and commented: "Its amazing that governments never learn." Twelve court challenges were launched, and a Federal Court has allowed the six from First Nations to proceed on an expedited basis. The Court also rejected challenges to the NEB's second approval and to the idea that Ottawa was in a conflict-of-interest.

Oddly Ottawa made no attempt to argue against the 12 challenges, prompting speculation that it is still lukewarm in its professed support for pipelines and expansion of oil sands production. Ottawa's response was that it will make its case for properly consulting when the six challenges go to court, a position that may reflect the fact that this is unfolding during an election campaign. In late August TMX gave its contractors 30 days to prepare for start-up. It remains to be seen whether the court will allow construction to proceed while the issue is before it.

It will take several months for the regulatory authorities to issue the necessary permits, so construction could begin in September though there is no guarantee that will happen before the October election. When construction begins, there is a possibility of civil disobedience and of violence by both First Nations and environmental groups. How the government responds can not be predicted, but the history of government handling of the Oka, Gustafsen Lake and Ipperwash incidents does not instill confidence.

Throughout this period the government and the settler community have continued the ancient game of "divide and conquer" by playing First Nation against each other and non-Indigenous Canadians against First Nations. This emerges in references to the fact that some First Nations approve the pipeline and some don't, that some are eager to buy shares in it, that First Nations are divided on the issue (as are non-Indigenous Canadians), and the impression being given that Ottawa has to consult with First Nations but not others (which the NEB does with its hearings), that First Nations are demanding a veto while non-Indigenous Canadians are not, or the suggestion that a pipeline cannot be built at all. Part of that is untrue and none of it is relevant to the validity of the concerns raised but it does divert attention from the real and legitimate need to consult properly with both First Nations and non-Indigenous Canadians.

The year 2019 opened with a new and different crisis over the question of consultations. Coastal GasLink, a subsidiary of TransCanada Corp, has BC government approval for a $40B project to deliver natural gas from northeast BC to Kitimat for shipment to Asia. It has negotiated approvals with 20 First Nations elected band councils along the 670 km route including the five band councils of the Wet'suwet'en nation. The negotiations did not include their hereditary Chiefs who have responsibility for safeguarding traditional rights to the large swaths of un-ceded territory that surround the reserves. These hereditary chiefs have opposed pipeline construction for 10 years including Northern Gateway and had erected a barricade about 300 km west of Prince George preventing Coastal GasLink employees from doing preliminary work for the proposed pipeline.

The fact that many people supported the traditional Chiefs called into question whether approval by the elected band councils represented meaningful consultations with the people in those five bands. The case of the Nak'azdli Whut'en band is informative. In a referendum 70% of the 300 members voted against the agreement but the council voted 4:3 to sign it. Those agreements are confidential, so their members and the public did not know what the council had accepted. That agreement was leaked, however, revealing that the council was to discourage members from criticizing the pipeline project, a clause that might violate the Charter of Rights.

In December, the BC Supreme Court issued an interim injunction to allow company employees to work in the disputed territory, and on January 7, the RCMP arrived to dismantle the barricade. They did so and arrested 14 people, charges that were later dropped for lack of evidence. They excluded the media, which could arouse suspicion from anyone familiar with their handling of previous crisis such as Gustafsen Lake. Protests in sympathy with the demonstrators erupted in Vancouver, Toronto, and Montreal, and the one in Ottawa forced an embarrassed PM Trudeau to postpone and then move the venue of a meeting with First Nations Chiefs. Subsequent negotiations have avoided further confrontations and allowed the workers temporary access. The RCMP have promised an investigation into allegations of the excessive use of force, but First Nations and others have little reason to trust such internal investigations.

A month later work was proceeding on pre-construction, and the hereditary Chiefs had submitted several complaints to the RCMP some of which could involve non-compliance with the company's permits. Since investigations of such complaints can be lengthy, the Chiefs called for a stop-work order. In July 2019 GasLink admitted that it had cleared land along the route without doing archeological assessments as required by its permits. In September hereditary Chiefs complained that a trail containing graves of warriors had been cleared before archeological work had been done and construction was suspended.

This situation is complicated by the fact that the elected leaders who have been consulted and gave approval are dependent on Ottawa for funding are only responsible for the reserve land. The hereditary Chiefs represent the much larger traditional territory, and they are the ones who won the famous 1996 Delgamuukw land claim agreement before the Supreme Court which covers that larger area. They also have significant support from the people as the demonstrations indicated. The claims by companies and governments that First Nations were consulted and gave consent are therefore less than accurate and do not necessarily reflect Supreme Court decisions. The issue also raises the question of what the federal government really means by its oft-stated support for "Reconciliation" when there is a real matter to be reconciled by action, decision, and supporting First Nations and not just words and promises to listen and "do what's best." At the time of writing, the future of consultations and pipelines in BC remains undecided.

On August 29, 2018, the federal government was taken by surprise by the Court's rejection of the Trans Mountain pipeline approval. The reason it was taken by surprise is that when it comes to dealing with Indigenous peoples it still refuses to learn from history, honour treaties, obey its own laws, or accept court decisions. The history speaks for itself. The following incidents resulted from Ottawa failing to consult or refusing to listen: the 1870 Red River Resistance, the 1885 Northwest Rebellion, the disastrous 1969 White Paper, the rejection of the MacKenzie River Valley Pipeline, the initial failure to patriate the BNA Act in 1982, the failure of the Meech Lake and Charlottetown Accords, the Oka crisis, Harper's education policy, numerous failed policy initiatives, thousands of projects on reserves, probably hundreds of thousands of administrative decisions by non-Indigenous DIA officials, the 2016 rejection of approval for the Northern Gateway pipeline, the 2018 rejection of approval for the Trans Mountain pipeline, and controversies over legislation in 2019 affecting child welfare, languages, and rights.

Ottawa has yet to develop satisfactory processes for consulting First Nations on the hundreds of issues that require meaningful consultations. But there has been progress since the days when the Department of Indian Affairs saw no reason to consult at all, a reflection of settler attitude towards First Nations, a reflection of colonialism.

Chapter 16

Land Claims, Court Decisions, New Treaties, and Indigenous Rights

France and England did not conquer or buy Canada from the peoples who inhabited it and neither did the government of Canada when it inherited British rights to the Dominion. Governments signed several treaties with various First Nations which cleared the way for white settlement, but the treaties did not transfer "sovereignty" over the land to Canada. For First Nations, the Creator is sovereign, and He allows them to use it. A First Nation would own their land or territory which was differentiated from that of another nation, but the Creator remained sovereign and they respected that sovereignty. For Europeans and non-Indigenous Canadians, governments are sovereign over land and land is owned by the governments, individuals, or companies.

Many of the treaties provided for land to be reserved for First Nations but the government then failed to honour many of those commitments. The result is that across Canada, many First Nations have claims to the land they believe is still theirs. Many of those claims have gone to the courts for settlement. Others have been settled through negotiation. The relationship between Canada and its First Nations includes several new "treaties" which are called agreements. They are having a significant impact on Canada and its First Nations population and on economic development. But hundreds of claims are still outstanding, obstacles to addressing poverty, economic development and the relationship between First Nations and non-Indigenous Canadians. Sadly, the process of addressing them is painfully slow.

After the fiasco of the 1969 White Paper and the Supreme Court decision on the Nisga'a land claim (the Calder case outlined below), Prime Minister Pierre Trudeau abandoned the plan to extinguish First Nations title to land through legislation and accepted that it had to be handled through negotiations. Ottawa offered assistance with land claims and appointed one commissioner with a limited mandate. It was a half-hearted beginning. The Office of Native Claims (ONC) was created in 1974 and put in charge of the process. It advanced money for research and legal fees and the bands then made their claims. The ONC decided if the claim was worth negotiating, and if so, it then negotiated on behalf of the government. If the claim was approved, the money advanced for research and other costs was deducted from the settlement.

The agreement was administered by the ONC which was essentially in a conflict of interest throughout the process. It took a narrow view of claims, refused to accept oral evidence which was a major basis for many claims, and did not have to give reasons for rejecting a claim. Unlike the First Nations, it had unlimited funds for lawyers. It was in the government's interest to settle as few claims as possible, to pay as little as possible, and to delay as long as possible, and that was the history of the ONC and its successor agencies. Indeed, the first settlement under this formal process, that with the Tsihlqot'in in BC, came in 2014, 40 years after it was launched.

In 1980, Ottawa issued a new policy on claims under the title "In all Fairness." This was an Orwellian use of language as the policy was anything but fair. There were no consultations, the government established the rules, and a major goal was the same as the ill-fated 1969 White Paper, namely, to turn common reserve land into private property. The ONC was replaced by two agencies, the Comprehensive Claims Branch and the Specific Claims Branch, but the number of unsettled claims kept increasing. By 1981, twelve had been settled and 250 were waiting for consideration. A decade later there were almost 400 claims under consideration - First Nations were reluctant to sign because of a clause requiring the renunciation of future claims. At the time negotiations were then underway to identify rights guaranteed by the new 1982 Charter of Rights and Section 35, so signing a land claim meant declining access to rights that the courts or governments might make available in the future.

In 1991, the Indian Claims Commission (ICC) was established to review appeals but it had little power and was terminated in 2009. The main feature of the settlements that have emerged is that First Nations receive land or money, the latter sometimes being designated to buy land from willing sellers. In return, they recognize the Crown's sovereignty over the land. The First Nation has therefore accepted in effect that the "settlers" are here to stay and that the federal and provincial governments have ultimate jurisdiction and power (sovereignty). The agreements may include a clause stating that in case of a conflict between laws passed by a band council and federal or provincial law, the latter prevail, which also implies the acceptance of Canadian sovereignty. It is also clear that Ottawa has not recognized any right of "self-determination," in the sense of national independence or sovereignty.

While this process was slowly evolving, First Nations were increasingly turning to the courts to settle their claims. Such cases often set important precedents, and it has been the courts rather than government that have led the way in settling land claims and establishing the rules. One of the first and most important was that of the James Bay Cree. The government of Quebec wanted to develop the enormous hydro-electric potential of James Bay and thought that it could do so without making arrangements with the people who had lived in the area for thousands of years.

In 1972, nine Cree bands in northern Quebec plus the Inuit obtained a court injunction to stop construction and that forced negotiations with Quebec City, Ottawa, and Quebec Hydro. The result was one of the most important agreements in Canadian history and the first "treaty" since 1921. The Cree surrendered title to 400,000 square miles but got title to 2,140 plus $140M over 10 years, control of land not flooded, recognition of traditional hunting and fishing rights, and some guarantees of environmental protection. There was an important self-government component – some control over taxation, services, infrastructure and affairs, that is, some escape from the Indian Act. Quebec got mineral rights subject to First Nations veto, and one of the largest hydro projects in the world was built. As with many such agreements it was criticized on both sides for being too generous or too stingy. Whether it was fairly implemented has been a matter of dispute.

At the same time, one of the most important cases was developing on the west coast, that of the Nisga'a First Nation in the Nass valley in northern BC. They had asked for a treaty in the 1850s, had never given up on the quest, and in 1967 one of their leaders, Frank Calder, took up the cause. He was one of the new leaders that governments were beginning to face and perhaps fear - well educated and experienced, an MLA for 26 years and a former cabinet minister.

The claim was that Nisga'a title to land had never been lawfully extinguished. This was an important point since there were no treaties covering mainland BC except for the northeast corner. In 1969, a BC court ruled that BC laws overruled whatever rights the Nisga'a might have had before contact. In 1973, six Supreme Court judges said the Nisga'a did have rights, the first time such rights had been recognized. The Court then divided 3-3 on whether subsequent acts of government had extinguished those rights. Later the Supreme Court voted 6:1 to recognize the rights.

The Calder case set an extremely important precedent and made way for the first agreement (or treaty) in BC since the 1850s. In the 1996 agreement, the Nisga'a got 2,000 square kilometers of the 25,000 they claimed, $200M, and a share of the local fishery but they lost their traditional tax exemption. The Nisga'a also obtained a degree of self government with the caveats that in case of conflict, federal or provincial law would prevail except on matters of their cultural, language, government, or citizenship. There was strong opposition to the terms, but it was ratified by a 51% vote in 1999. Other bands in BC did not view it as a good deal and only four have since made similar agreements.

In Vancouver, a dispute over the value of a tiny piece of land produced important precedents. The DIA administers reserve land allegedly in the interests of its inhabitants, and in 1956 it leased 65 hectares of the Musqueam reserve in Vancouver to a golf club. DIA apparently did not keep the band council properly informed of the negotiations, and in 1975 chief Delbert Guerin claimed that DIA had charged far less than the market value. The courts agreed and awarded the reserve $10M. The decision also established that the Royal Proclamation of 1763 applied to the whole of Canada, a matter of considerable importance as the Proclamation had recognized Indian sovereignty over land west of Quebec but the boundaries of that land were unclear. The case, known as Guerin, also established that DIA was legally liable for the administration (or misuse) of reserve assets in the interests of First Nations.

Some of the most important agreements have been made in the North because there is a far higher proportion of Indigenous people in the population, resource development is so important to the Canadian economy, and Ottawa's imprint is so recent and light that oral memories of agreements are still fresh. As a result, Ottawa needs agreements and the Indigenous peoples are in a far better bargaining position than those elsewhere in Canada. In the Yukon, negotiations with 14 nations began in the 1970s. By 1992-3, a Framework Agreement had been signed which all 14 must use for their own specific agreements. Four nations signed at the time, seven signed later. They have received money, land, participation in management bodies for resources, hunting and fishing rights, protection of culture, a share of revenue from resources, a degree of self-government and some protection for the environment. As usual the agreement has been criticized from all sides.

A crucial court case cited in the literature is the one called Delgamuukw. In 1987, 48 hereditary Chiefs of the Gitsan and Wet'suwet'em bands in northwestern BC claimed 58,000 square kilometers of land. The case took four years and they lost. In 1997, the Supreme Court reversed that ruling with a significant decision. It stated that oral evidence was admissible, overturning a century of Ottawa's previously successful definition of treaties as containing only the written words and not the oral promises made to obtain the Chiefs' signatures. The decision clarified Aboriginal title and the government's duty to consult them on issues affecting them. It is highly significant that this settlement was with hereditary Chiefs rather than elected ones, and it covered traditional territories far greater than the reserves. That is the area of the current dispute over the $40B Coastal GasLink pipeline.

One of the smallest land claims has been one of the most explosive in terms of politics, violence and symbolism, namely a few acres of land beside the town of Oka northwest of Montreal. The dispute dates back centuries when Mohawks were invited to settle on land France had granted to the Sulpician religious order. France refused to recognize Mohawk title to the land they had settled on and the British maintained the French position. The first claim was rejected in 1781, and the issue led to violence and arrests in the nineteenth century. By 1912, rival claims of the village of Oka and the Kanesatake were in the courts but no solution emerged. In 1950, the town built a golf course near a Mohawk cemetery, and more Mohawk land claims were rejected in the 1970s.

In 1990, Oka decided to expand the golf course into the cemetery and Mohawk warriors occupied the site. On July 11, police attacked the Mohawks and one policeman was killed. During the three-month standoff Ottawa sent 2,500 troops who outnumbered the entire reserve population. Other Mohawks and First Nations joined and the crucial Mercier bridge at Montreal was blockaded, a reflection of decades of frustration on the Kahnawake Reserve on the south shore of the St. Lawrence River. With the Charter of Rights only eight years old, soldiers blatantly interfered with fundamental rights including movement, assembly, and speech.

The crisis resulted from decades if not centuries of neglect, insensitivity, over-reaction, and the ultimate exhaustion of patience. At the last moment, Ottawa and Quebec City backed down from a potentially needless bloodbath but the incident cost them $200M, the golf course did not get the land, and Canada's international reputation was tarnished. Many Canadians also questioned the federal and provincial government's handling of the issue.

Two Mohawks were sentenced to jail, 39 were released. The Mulroney government responded as governments often do - it shelved the issue by appointing the Royal Commission on Aboriginal Peoples (RCAP). It produced a huge report six years later dealing with a wide range of issues, a report that was essentially ignored. A decade later, Ottawa signed an agreement giving the Mohawks control of 960 hectares of land, but the overall issues were still not resolved.

In July 2019 a developer, Grégoire Collin, offered to gift 60 hectares of land to the band and sell another 150 hectares to Ottawa to give to the band. A few days later Oka mayor Pascal Quevillon cast a chill over that positive development by suggesting that the land would house more garbage dumps and illegal cigarette and pot shops and lower property values. He does not seem to understand that towns have no voice in how reserve land is used and vice versa, which is why reserves were created in the first place. He refused to apologize for comments some regard as racist. He also complained that Oka would be surrounded by the reserve, a situation First Nations understand as all their reserves are surrounded by non-Indigenous land. Mayor Quevillon warned of a second Oka crisis but Chief Serge Simon said that will not happen. On August 6 Oka town council asked Ottawa to suspend talks with the Mohawks and send the RCMP to the reserve. Grand Chief Simon replied that the town of Oka has no jurisdiction on the reserve. Interestingly the town's tourist map does not show the golf course, the cemetery, or the border between town, reserve, and disputed territory!

New urban reserves have become another means of solving land claims. The federal government violated terms in Treaty 1 that set aside lands in Manitoba, and several nations claimed they had been cheated out of 1.423 million acres of land. The claim was accepted in 1991, and the question was how to right the wrong since all the relevant area had long been settled by whites. A solution was at hand, namely the Kapyong military base in southwest Winnipeg which became available in 2004 when the army left it unoccupied. First Nations wanted it as an urban reserve on which they could develop various economic enterprises to deal with their poverty.

Instead of cooperating or engaging in consultations, Ottawa tried to sell it or divide it and engaged in a series of tactics to avoid using it to settle the claim. First Nations went to court, the only avenue that seemed to work for them. In 2007, the Manitoban government agreed. Eleven years later, in April 2018, Ottawa agreed, and the transfer was finally signed on September 1, 2019. More and more urban reserves are cropping up in cities such as Saskatoon which now has six, Winnipeg, and Brandon. There are now at least 130, some tiny satellites of reserves, and the number is rapidly increasing.

In Ontario, an agreement in principle was signed with the Algonquins on October 18, 2016, covering cash plus 36,000 square kilometers of land between Ottawa and North Bay. This followed 24 years of negotiations and is the first modern treaty in Ontario. The development of the abandoned Rockcliffe airbase in Ottawa will provide part of the funding for the settlement. That deal is complicated by the question raised in Chapter 1 - who are the Status Indians who can vote to ratify it? The Iroquois and others have challenged it. Across the river, Ottawa has provided the Kitigan Zibi First Nations in Maniwaki $116M to purchase an additional 363 acres for their reserve.

In Saskatchewan, 29 bands claimed that promised land had never been provided - in 1992 they received $500M to buy 1.3 million acres. Land is not the only issue - in 1984 the Blackfoot in Alberta received $1,675,000 for cattle that had not been delivered a century earlier. In January 2019, Ottawa reached agreement with Alberta's Blood band to provide $150M in compensation for the mismanagement of their cattle between 1894 and 1923. The claim was launched in 2000 and accepted in 2011. The amount was negotiated over five years, the deal settled in March 2019, and was signed in July. On June 12, 2019 the Federal Court ordered Ottawa to give the same band 258 square kilometers of land that had not been included in the original reserve in 1877 due to underestimating the population. That case had taken 23 years and the band urged Ottawa not to appeal the decision. In July 2019 Ottawa gave the Katlodeedhe band in the NWT $28.3M for livestock and equipment that was never delivered when Treaty 8 was signed in 1900.

Another major leap forward for First Nations was the settlement of the Tsilhqot'in claim to 440,000 square kilometers of land around Williams Lake, BC. The case began in 1992 when inhabitants blockaded a road to stop logging companies operating on land they claimed as theirs. On June 26, 2014, the Supreme Court voted 8-0 to grant them 1,700 square kilometers. However, for the first time the Court recognized their title to the land, a precedent and landmark ruling that could apply to many Indigenous claims. They cannot veto economic development, but it requires their consent or proof by the government that the project is essential and that the bands have been properly compensated. Companies can harvest the forests and build pipelines, but they must obtain the consent of the people who own the land. By 2015, 65 negotiations had been completed or were underway covering 104 of BC's 203 bands.

On the prairies, land was taken from the reserves such as that of the Kahkewistahaw east of Regina. It was surveyed in 1881, but white settlers soon began attempting to buy the good parts. That was resisted until 1906 when the band was starving, without a chief, and one member signed a sale in violation of the Indian Act. In 1989, the reserve launched a claim which Ottawa settled in 2002 for $94.6M.

Fighting these claims has cost First Nations hundreds of millions of dollars which the government loaned to them and then deducted from the settlements. The 2018 budget indicated that Ottawa would pay the costs of negotiating future ones but not previous ones, a welcome half-step forward and a new double standard. Now Ottawa is paying all these costs. One-by-one the claims are being settled, one of the latest being a payment of almost $3M for 4 acres of land that should have been included in the Beecher Bay reserve near Victoria in 1878.

In October 2018, one of the great injustices of the 1880s was finally resolved after decades of negotiation. When Treaty 8 was signed the Lubicon Lake Cree were left out making them "non-Indians" and hence ineligible for the rights others won when whites settled the prairies. That became a major issue when oil was discovered on their land. Finally, Ottawa and Alberta reached a settlement - recognition of their occupation of 246 square kilometers of land and $113M in compensation.

Even when claims are settled, implementation can take decades. According to a 1997 agreement the federal government was to give 21 Manitoba First Nations 445,000 hectares of land that had been promised in the treaties but never allocated. By 2019 only 215,000 hectares had been delivered. The agreement required the First Nations to accept that they would take no more legal actions. They are now asking the courts to release them from that obligation so they can sue Ottawa for failing to deliver the land.

The treaties promised First Nations that they could continue hunting and fishing on the lands they were ceding that were not occupied or used by settlers. Gradually the federal and provincial governments whittled down those rights with serious effects on health and income. In the last four decades, several court decisions reversed the trend and rights to hunting and fishing have gradually expanded. In 1980, RCMP charged James Simon with possessing a rifle in violation of Nova Scotian law. He argued that the 1752 Peace Treaty gave the Mi'kmaq the right to hunt, and the Supreme Court agreed in 1985. In 1984, Ronald Sparrow was charged in BC with using a fishing net larger than the ones permitted. Two lower courts found him guilty, the next overturned that decision, and in 1990 the Supreme Court upheld the acquittal.

In the 1996 Adams case, a Mohawk won the right to fish in a Quebec lake contrary to provincial law. In 1999, the Supreme Court acquitted Donald Marshall of catching and selling eels out of season in violation of the Fisheries Act. But many other problems such as fishing for lobster in the Maritimes remain unresolved. In 2015, Kristjan Pierone killed a moose on unused land in Saskatchewan and was charged with unlawful hunting. The charge was dismissed, then upheld, then dismissed, so Saskatchewan took it to the Supreme Court where it lost.

White man's governments are certainly tenacious. In January 2019 a 16-month sting operation was successfully concluded when a

Saskatchewan conservation officer posing as a scientist exchanged tobacco for $90 worth of fish from Donald Iron of the Canoe Lake Band. Chief Bobby Cameron of the Federation of Sovereign Indigenous Nations pointed out that fishing was legal under the treaties and wondered why the government's resources were not directed to serious crime such as the opioid crisis, domestic violence, and drunk driving. Details were sketchy because the sting operation was covered by a publication ban but the CBC succeeded in getting part of the ban lifted. Saskatchewan remains persistent and is now considering a law to make it more difficult for First Nations to hunt on private property that is not being farmed, a right granted in the treaties.

Many of these issues relate to the rights First Nations were guaranteed in principle in Section 35 of the 1982 Constitution. That Section did not identify specific rights which was to be done in a series of meetings between Indigenous leaders and the prime minister and premiers. Meetings were held in 1982, 1983, 1984, and 1987, but they failed to produce agreement. Court cases then began filling in the blanks and clarifying the rights of First Nations to land, consultation, self-government, religious and cultural activities, and hunting and fishing.

On February 14, 2018, Prime Minister Trudeau announced a plan to identify the rights covered by Section 35 of the Constitution, draft the necessary legislation by Christmas, and have it passed before the 2019 election. This would turn the post-1982 court decisions into law and fulfill recommendations made in the RCAP report of 1995. The legislation would emerge from consultations with Indigenous groups, the provinces and the territories. Given that the previous effort failed over five years and that Trudeau was proposing to resolve the problems of 150 years of colonialism in 18 months, the announcement was greeted with considerable scepticism.

Questions quickly emerged: why not enforce existing treaties, why not settle existing land claims, why insist that settlements include a commitment to renounce future claims, and what evidence was there that the provinces were now in favour? The framework was advertised as a means to ensure Ottawa fulfilled agreements, suggesting that without another agreement Ottawa would continue its 150-year record of violating existing ones! It was criticized for not providing self-government and for failure to meet the standards of UNDRIP or the existing constitution. With only months left in the mandate, this issue looked like another promise likely to be broken.

On August 21, Chief Wilton Littlechild of Treaty 6 and two other Chiefs wrote the Prime Minister saying that the process was backwards because it was the First Nations that should be identifying their rights, not the government. In September, the government released a framework document after five months of consultations, a document which became a major issue at the annual AFN meeting that month. The government's approach was condemned by several Chiefs particularly on the grounds that it did not deal with land and resources; it did not cover the role of the provinces or the agreements reached after 1921; and it was government-driven, moving too fast, and insufficiently transparent. The post-1982 meetings came to grief partly because of the opposition of the provinces so it was far from clear how meaningful the new initiative could be without their full participation and agreement.

Opposition continued to grow. In October the Association of Iroquois and Allied Indians said the proposed framework would reduce rights and should be opposed in the next federal election. It also become clear that there were serious disagreements between then Justice Minister Jody Wilson-Raybould and Minister of Crown-Indigenous Relations Carolyn Bennett. Wilson-Raybould had worked on the issues for years before entering politics and then as Minister and Attorney General. She believed her department had the expertise to begin drafting the bill. Bennett wanted to begin with consultations. Bennett won the battle but lost the war because First Nations did not agree with the process. The Indigenous Rights legislation has been shelved but work continues on elements in it such as revisions to land claims, self-government, and treaty negotiations. The AFN continues to oppose the entire process on the grounds that it should be driven by First Nations and not the government.

Since the James Bay agreement, 26 "comprehensive" treaties have been negotiated covering 40% of Canada's land surface. Nine are called "modern treaty agreements" because they include provisions for limited self-government which free the bands from some of the provisions of the Indian Act. Indigenous peoples obtained control of 600,000 square kilometers of that, $3.2B in compensation, nation-to-nation agreements with the federal government, and some transfer of power to bands. But

75 were still outstanding, mainly in BC. By 2016 1,222 of the approximately 1,713 "specific" land claims filed since 1973 had been settled and only 138 were still active, a major leap forward. The Supreme Court has ruled on 40 cases relating to Section 35 of the Constitution, usually on the side of First Nations.

Arthur Ray, who gave expert advice for several land claims cases, provided part of the explanation for the ineffectiveness, slowness and cost of the process. In 1989, Alberta's Samson Cree claimed Treaty 6 had been violated. The case was settled in 2005 at a cost to the two sides of $100M. It had involved 365 trial days with dozens of lawyers and expert witnesses, and thousands of documents. That First Nation is rich; most others cannot afford clean drinking water let alone a fifteen-year court battle with the federal government.

Canada's response to the United Nations Declaration on the Rights of Indigenous Peoples (UNDRIP) underlines how backward and out-of-step the country is with the rest of the world. When the Declaration was adopted in 2007 by a vote of 143 to 4, the four included Canada, the US, Australia, and New Zealand, all English-speaking countries with colonized Indigenous populations. The Trudeau government promised to adopt it. In May 2016, Minister Bennett said Canada would fully endorse it, but then in July Minister Wilson-Raybould said it could not be implemented under Canadian law. It would expand Indigenous rights beyond whatever is promised in Section 35 of the Constitution, but how far is unclear. One example is that UNDRIP says that the "consent" of Indigenous peoples is needed for resource development (and pipelines) but there is dispute as to whether that means having a veto.

Early in 2018, NDP MP Romeo Saganash, who is Cree, introduced a private member's bill calling on Canada to harmonize its laws with UNDRIP. Such bills have little chance of succeeding, but this one continued to move through the Commons and Senate procedures obtaining widespread support but opposition from Conservative MPs and Senators. It did not receive approval before the autumn election. In February British Columbia became the first province to announce that it would implement UNDRIP. The details will be fascinating and extremely important, because no province has more land claims problems, and the approvals for both the Kinder Morgan and the Pacific GasLink pipelines seem to fall short of UNDRIP standards.

Ottawa's record in dealing with claims under the Specific Claims program has been monitored by the BC Specific Claims Working Group. In November 2018, it stated that two-thirds of the claims filed between January 1, 2014 and November 10, 2015, had not been dealt with within the governments three-year deadline as required by the relevant Act. What they were getting, they said, was "a lot of rhetoric, a lot of promises, and they are very hollow..." A letter sent to the federal government from the Union of BC Chiefs in November 2018 said: "Non-compliance with legislation...contradicts every public commitment your government has made regarding reconciliation."

On December 4, Minister Bennett announced that the system would be improved but there was a lack of consensus amongst First Nations on how to proceed. On September 5, 2019, Ottawa, BC, and 65 BC First Nations signed an agreement to speed up the negotiating process. The main changes are that Ottawa accepts First Nations rights so that issue is no longer in dispute and all three are equal parties at the talks. But half of BC's First Nations are not part of the agreement, and many have overlapping territorial claims with those that are so it is not clear how permanent an agreement can be.

Those claims and other rights issues must be addressed for the good of First Nations, Canadians in general, and the country's economic development and reputation. Doing so is a matter of commitment, effort and money, and it is one of the crucial points at which the vicious circles of the "Indian problem" can be broken. Addressing other rights issues as PM Trudeau promised to do in February 2018, is also essential, but the land claims are concrete, and many have been outstanding for decades. The Oka crisis was over a tiny parcel of land, but it left a huge legacy: First Nations patience is not inexhaustible. Some solutions are not that difficult. Nine-tenths of Canadian land belongs to the Crown, only 0.2% is in reserves, and much of that Crown land borders on reserves in remote areas. Giving some of it back would help break the colonial legacy at little or no cost at all.

Chapter 17

Reconciliation and Political Correctness

One thing that annoys First Nations is walking past statues of one of the people they regard as responsible for "colonialism," for the residential schools, the suppression of their ancestors, the theft of their land or other injustices of the past. Another thing is using a building, street or bridge named after such a person. Statues are erected for these people because they occupy a significant place in Canada's non-Indigenous history but paradoxically, they occupy a place of infamy in Canada's Indigenous history. Reconciling those two histories is a challenge Canadians have only begun to address.

The Truth and Reconciliation Commission made 94 recommendations for how Canadians could right the wrongs of the residential school tragedy but removing statues and renaming objects was not one of them. However, that Commission succeeded in launching Indigenous and non-Indigenous Canadians on their own paths to reconciliation and, in effect, Canadians invented a 95th recommendation. For them, true reconciliation will not take place if Canadians continue to celebrate the people responsible for the tragic history of Indigenous peoples without also acknowledging the wrongs done by those heroes.

The movement to rename buildings and remove statues has been quite spontaneous. A particular name or statue will be identified or perhaps has been controversial for decades. Pressure grows to have it removed or renamed. There may be a debate in government and the media. Decisions are made and there are winners and losers. And the whole issue has sparked a great and useful debate about Canadian history, the writing and revising of history, how to handle the record of flawed politicians, judging the past through the lens of the present and, of course, the hero/villains themselves.

At least half a dozen Canadians are facing the forces of revision. The most controversial name in play is that of Sir John A. Macdonald. There are many statues of Sir John A. and many buildings named after him because he was, of course, one of the chief architects of Confederation and the first Prime Minister. From 1867 to 1892, he played a major role in developing the residential school system and other policies that affected First Nations. For that reason, there is considerable pressure to remove statues and rename buildings which, of course, runs into the opposition of those who believe Canada should acknowledge his outstanding contribution with those statues and buildings and, indeed, that there should be more of them.

In August 2017, the Ontario Union of Elementary School Teachers passed a resolution calling for the renaming of all the Sir John A. Macdonald schools in the province. That touched off a lively debate. Assembly of First Nations Grand Chief Perry Bellegarde said that being in a school named after Macdonald would make an Indigenous student uneasy. The province's then Premier Kathleen Wynne opposed it and former federal cabinet minister John Baird said it was "simply trying to erase history." That was a false argument – naming a building after someone does not "create" history so removing it does not "erase" history. An Angus Reid poll showed 55% opposed to changing the name and 25% in favour, and no name changes have yet been made.

More successful was the campaign to remove a statue of Sir John from the entrance to the City Hall in Victoria, BC. The argument was that in order to do business with their government, Indigenous people had to walk past a statue of their ancestors' oppressor. A committee was struck, it worked with Indigenous peoples on the issue of reconciliation, it recommended that the statue be moved elsewhere, and Council voted 7:1 to remove it.

It was an ironic decision because Council postponed deciding where to put the statue so Macdonald will be in storage temporarily. They thus made "disappear" the man whose policies were designed to make Indigenous people "disappear." Many of the 94 recommendations of the Truth and Reconciliation Commission are substantive and expensive - removing this statue was symbolic and cheap. The real colonial past in BC's provincial capital is reflected in the city's name itself because Queen Victoria presided over the conquest of a large part of the world and the suppression of millions of Indigenous people, but the city's name remains unchanged while lesser steps have been taken such as putting First Nations names on a new library and some streets.

Macdonald's residential school policy was implemented by his Minister of the Interior, Hector-Louis Langevin, one of the most important French-Canadian Father of Confederation and main builders of the new Dominion. To honour him, the building opposite Parliament which houses the Prime Minister's office was named the Langevin Block. In 2017, First Nations began a campaign to have it renamed. On June 21, 2017, Prime Minister Justin Trudeau made it the Office of the Prime Minister and Privy Council. This act of "political correctness" raised the question of a Liberal government removing a Conservative name from a prominent public building, an act of politically tainted reconciliation.

Like many other issues of political correctness, renaming the Langevin Block was open to the charge of hypocrisy. Macdonald's and Langevin's policy was certainly designed to make the First Nations "disappear," but it only affected a portion of the school-age population. Prime Minister Pierre Trudeau's 1969 White Paper was designed to make the entire First Nations population "disappear," and do so in a modern period of liberalism unlike Macdonald's period of imperialism and white supremacy. So how could Justin Trudeau remove Langevin's name from a building in Ottawa and leave the name of his father, Pierre Elliott Trudeau, on Montreal's international airport?

The association of Macdonald alone with the residential schools is also a misreading of history. There were schools in New France designed to "civilize" First Nations. Is Laval University to be renamed? The first of the nineteenth-century schools was established in Ontario in 1831 and there were a number in operation before Confederation. Macdonald expanded the system until his death in 1891 but it matured under Liberal Prime Minister Sir Wilfrid Laurier from 1896 to 1911 when far more students attended each year. It continued under prime ministers up to Jean Chrétien. Some articles mention that Macdonald's policy affected 150,000 students which is true, but most of them went to the schools under Liberal Prime Ministers.

The contortions that political correctness can create are well illustrated by the strange case of an individual who decided in 2013 to have statues made of all 22 Prime Ministers and donate them to a park in Kitchener, Ontario. Kitchener city council agreed but then changed its mind when pressure mounted to exclude the statue of Macdonald. Sir Wilfrid Laurier University in nearby Waterloo agreed to host the collection in 2015 but then surrendered to a similar outcry. So, a university named for a Liberal Prime Minister whose government hosted far more students in residential schools than Macdonald's would not host a statue of a Conservative Prime Minister whose government hosted far fewer. In 2016, the statues found a resting place in the nearby town of Baden.

Elsewhere in Canada Macdonald's statues and name are under siege. He survives in Victoria Park in Regina, but has been painted green with his hands painted red. In 2017, then Premier Brad Wall called the campaign to remove the statue a "slippery slope." The Canadian Historical Association has also adopted the ways of political correctness with its prestigious "Sir John A. Macdonald Prize" becoming the "Best Scholarly Book in Canadian History" by a vote of 121 to 11. Trust historians to make history boring.

One man who played an important role in the development of the residential schools was Egerton Ryerson, widely regarded as the father of modern education in the province of Ontario. The system reflected his views and those of the time, namely that First Nations had to be assimilated, that the residential schools were the means to do it, and that would require making them different from other schools. In 2017, activists at Ryerson University in Toronto demanded that the name be changed. Their views were heard and examined, the name was not changed, and the University issued a detailed explanation of Ryerson's role and of its position on changing names.

On the east coast, the most controversial issue was the removal of a statue of Edward Cornwallis from a park in Halifax. Cornwallis was the founder and governor of Halifax, a noted military and political figure in the history of the city and the province. In the 1930s, a large statue was erected to commemorate his contributions. However, during the wars in 1749, he offered a bounty for the scalps of Mi'kmaq who were allies of the French. Because of that, the Mi'kmaq had long demanded that the statue be removed.

It was a difficult decision for the city council. He was, after all, the founder of their city. There was no question that he had issued the bounty offer, but it was standard practice at the time, the French had done it, and Mi'kmaq warriors had sold English scalps to the French. A public opinion poll found 56% in favour of keeping the statue, but the city decided to remove it. Less successful was the campaign to remove the name of General Jeffrey Amherst from a park in PEI on the alleged grounds that he ordered blankets containing smallpox germs to be distributed to First Nations. It is questionable that he did so, and the park has not been renamed. He suffered a worse fate in Montreal when his name disappeared from a street and a campaign is underway in Ottawa to make his name disappear from a street.

On the west coast several issues have arisen in addition to moving the Macdonald statue in Victoria. In 1864, seven Tsilhgot'in chiefs were hung for killing 14 whites who had invaded their territory. The chiefs had been tricked into entering negotiations, and the executions had always been viewed as a grave injustice by their people. The BC Law Society removed from their premises a statue of Sir Matthew Begbie, the judge who presided over that trial. That was controversial as he apparently carried out his duties according to the law and was viewed at the time as a fair, liberal, and pro-Indigenous judge. He has also disappeared from the grounds of the New Westminster provincial courthouse. In March 2018, Prime Minister Justin Trudeau apologized for the 1864 hanging and in November he apologized again.

In June 2017, the University of Victoria removed the name of Joseph Trutch, the first Lieutenant Governor of the province, from a student residence. He had certainly played a role in trampling the rights of Indigenous peoples, and their descendants would have felt uneasy living in a residence named after him. On the other coast, the University of New Brunswick law school is under pressure to remove the name of George Ludlaw from its main hall. He was the colony's first chief justice but supported residential schools.

Other examples of name changing abound, some controversial, some not. In May 2018, the Ontario Art Gallery changed the name of Emily Carr's famous 1929 painting "Indian Church" to "The Church at Yuquot Village." This raised the question of interfering with an artist's work or words to achieve political correctness. In June 2018, the government of Newfoundland and Labrador launched a project to remove the word "savage" from the wording of its 1637 coat-of-arms. The province is also considering changing the name of its provincial holiday from "Discovery Day" since Cabot definitely did not discover the island. Pressure is mounting in Saskatchewan to change the name of a road honouring Edgar Dewdney, the Indian Commissioner who withheld rations to force people onto reserves.

In August 2018, the Bank of Montreal in old Montreal removed plaques that referred to the founder of Montreal, Paul de Chomedey, Sieur de Maisonneuve, killing a chief "with his own hands," plaques that did not mention that the chief was defending his land. The changes go down to the local level - in 2019 the town of Mitchell, Manitoba, renamed its Mohawk hockey team at an estimated cost of $20,000 as "the right thing to do." On April 12 McGill University dropped the controversial name "Redmen" from its male sports teams. In Orillia, Ontario, a statue of Champlain is being reworked to remove four First Nations depicted sitting at the feet of priests and fur traders an implication of inferiority and subordination.

Winnipeg may have found a better way. There the city surveyed Indigenous peoples for their opinion about a boulevard named after a supporter of residential schools. Fourteen percent said leave it alone; 57% said leave it alone but do some education work about the namesake; and only 25% said change it. What they wanted was real progress on land claims and other important issues. Saskatoon now consults Indigenous leaders when drafting the wording for plaques on structures such as bridges.

Even commemorative days are subject to change. In June 2017, the government changed the name of National Aboriginal Day to National Indigenous Peoples Day to keep up with evolving views. That could be the day established as a national holiday of reconciliation if an NDP private members bill is accepted, and the government has said it will support it. That would fulfill recommendation #80 of the Truth and Reconciliation Commission, and AFN Grand Chief Perry Bellegarde is supporting it. The government assigned the former American Embassy on Wellington opposite Parliament as a cultural centre for Indigenous Peoples. It is difficult to believe that this resulted from "meaningful consultations" because the First Nations had demanded nearby Victoria Island in the Ottawa River, a place of ancient importance to them, while the Embassy carried the legacy of American colonialism and totally inappropriate architecture.

Given the responsibility of past leaders for the mistreatment of Indigenous peoples and the fact statues were made of them and objects named after them, one can expect continued pressure to remove the statues and change the names. Politics being what it is, one can also expect both support and opposition to such pressure for both good and bad motives. Proposed changes will remain controversial. Environment Minister Catherine McKenna who is responsible for Parks Canada has questioned the value of revisionism and has asked the Historic Sites and Monuments Board to look at how to handle the issue.

Opposition leader Andrew Scheer has stated that all leaders have flaws, and statues representing Sir John A. Macdonald "and his legacy should not be removed from public spaces..." Senator Murray Sinclair, Chairman of the TRC, said that pulling down statues is counterproductive to reconciliation and "smacks of revenge." Those advocating revisions should also remember that it can work both ways - the heroes of Indigenous peoples had flaws and one of them led the Red River Resistance and the Northwest Rebellion. Governments also need strong public support to deal with problems such as the poverty of Indigenous peoples and that is not helped by attacks on the heroes of large segments of the public. Perhaps rewriting history should be left to books like this.

Conclusion:

We Are All Treaty People; Where Do We Go From Here?

Canada is at a crossroads in terms of its relations with its First Nations. They know it, and more and more non-Indigenous Canadians know it. But many non-Indigenous Canadians do not know or understand the history of the treatment of the First Nations, the reasons for it, the policies, the basis for those policies or lack thereof, the injustices, and the racial discrimination that underlay so much of the policy. Above all, they do not understand that the effects of 150 years of colonialism are very much still with us. They are an enormous burden on our First Nations, but they are getting more and more attention partly because they are an enormous burden on the whole population.

The Chapter on myths is instructive – First Nations are not what many people think they are, Ottawa's claim to their land is questionable, and Canadians fool themselves if they think Canada was not a colonial power and is still not a colonial power. The power wielded by our government over First Nations today is clearly colonial, less oppressive than a year ago or a decade ago, much less than a century ago, but still discriminatory and essentially unacceptable.

In effect, Canada has been at this crossroads since Pierre Trudeau and Jean Chrétien introduced the infamous 1969 White Paper. That document was designed to complete the policy of assimilation begun in the 1830s and to finally eliminate any legal or constitutional rights or distinctions of First Nations peoples. It was to be the conclusion of a century long process of making Indians "disappear," of residential schools, cultural genocide, shrinking reserves, marginalization, the Sixties Scoop, discrimination, and poverty produced by deliberate government policies with all the inevitable effects of poverty – high mortality rates, disease, violence, high incarceration rates, abuse of all kinds. The government was marching in the same direction set out by Sir John A.

Macdonald and was now speeding up as it saw final victory on the immediate horizon.

First Nations were marching in exactly the opposite direction. For a century they had survived the onslaught on their culture, their identity, their unity, and their governance. Their population had fallen from around 500,000 at the time of contact to perhaps 100,000 by 1920, but it then stabilized and begun growing. After the Second World War it began growing faster than the Canadian average, a sign of cultural and political resilience. In a post-colonial world, with tens of thousands of veterans on the reserves, with human, women's and minority rights on the national agenda, with better education, with access to legal advice, and with better organization, First Nations were not to be ignored and manipulated as their ancestors had been.

First Nations were so outraged by the new assault on their identity and their rights that for the first time ever they united from coast to coast to oppose this very serious attempt to make them disappear. That itself proved that a century of divide-and-conquer policies had failed. Splitting nations into numerous bands, placing reserves far from each other, creating elected councils to undermine and compete with traditional councils, buying off leaders and organizations, these and other efforts had all ultimately failed.

The 1969 White Paper was the point in Canadian history when First Nations said they would never be assimilated, and they would never abandon their rights and reserves. They were here first, the meaning of "First Nations," a name they soon adopted for themselves They had never been conquered; they had never signed treaties of surrender; they and never accepted that they were "subjects" of the British or Canadian Crowns. They had agreed to "share" their land, either *de facto* as they were pushed off it in much of Canada, or *de jure* as they signed treaties sharing the land in return for financial and other forms of compensation and other rights. They had never accepted that sovereignty had passed from the Creator to the French, British, or Canadian governments.

Rather than make them disappear, the 1969 White Paper made them appear, in Ottawa in the hundreds, drawn from all across the country, united for the first time in a massive offensive to reverse the erosion of their power, rights and land, then to regain lost power, rights, and land. Given the balance of power between them and non-Indigenous Canadians and the fact that the latter had used and continued to use the full weight of government to impose its views, that has been a long and extremely difficult struggle. It is, indeed, only partly completed as today's land claims, consultations, inquiries, legal settlements, and confrontations make clear. But one mark of success is the fact that these issues are in the headlines on almost a daily basis, and the media coverage is often positive. Fifty years ago, if such issues even made the news, most would have been blamed on the "Indians" as is still the case for some issues such as stalled pipeline construction resulting from the government's failure to consult properly.

This book has documented many of the major strides First Nations have made since 1969. The first was creating a better organization to fight the White Paper; the second was success in forcing the government to officially abandon that policy. Governments then attempted to achieve the same goals by smaller steps, efforts that were also successfully blocked. Failure to consult First Nations about their future led to the postponement of Pierre Trudeau's plan to patriate the constitution, the addition of guarantees for Aboriginal rights to the Constitution, and the failure of PM Brian Mulroney's attempt to amend the constitution by addressing Quebec's grievances while postponing addressing those of Indigenous peoples. Those developments ensured that First Nations are now invited to heads-of-government meetings and consulted to a degree not dreamed of three decades ago.

For decades Canada has been attempting to come to grips with the legacy of its colonial past. Where exactly Canadians are along that road is impossible to estimate and is certainly a matter of personal opinion. The debate over apologies, renaming buildings and moving statues makes that very clear. The residential schools are gone, most victims compensated, and the 94 Calls for Action of the Truth and Reconciliation Commission are gradually being put into effect. The Sixties Scoop – adoption without consent leading to cultural genocide – is officially over but adoption continues on a daily basis, one of many things that governments are "working on."

The decades-old demand for an inquiry into missing and murdered women and girls was accepted by the Trudeau Liberals in 2015 and launched in 2016. It has been a text-book case in how not to handle a public inquiry. Its 231 Calls for Justice address all the issues but it does not add much to recommendations that have been made in the previous 98 studies of the same problems, It will add to the momentum to implement them. Meanwhile, there is no evidence that the rate of missing and murdered has declined. Several recent reports have been highly critical of racism in various police departments and the conditions that produce violence against Indigenous women are being addressed slowly at best.

The current government of Justin Trudeau has made more progress addressing First Nations problems than any previous one, arguably a completely different level and amount of progress. It stated that no relationship was more important than that with Indigenous peoples and set out to make that a reality. Budgets were substantially increased for all the relevant sectors – education, health, housing, welfare, and infrastructure. Much was made of an inexcusable situation, the absence of drinking water on reserves, and the number of boil-water advisories has fallen by 87 since 2015 with the remaining 57 to be removed by the deadline of March 2021.

There has also been substantial progress on issues like land claims, new treaties or agreements, and the devolution of more power from the DIA to reserve bands. But the record remains spotty. The incarceration rates for Indigenous Canadians are inexcusable and reflect the continuing effects of policies like the residential schools, the failed attempts at assimilation, adoption into non-Indigenous families, poverty, and especially 150 years of serious under-funding by governments on Indigenous people as compared to spending on the same services for the rest of the population. That gap is narrowing, but it has to be closed completely followed by years of additional work to deal with the continuing effects of underspending in past decades.

Serious problems remain in the relationship between governments and First Nations which is also the relationship between Indigenous and non-Indigenous Canadians. The Indian Act remains in force, including discrimination against women and the entire fact of colonialism, of a government based on a non-Indigenous population controlling many aspects of life of Indigenous ones. Most reserves do not have real "self-government," and it is hardly meaningful if funds are not available for the programs that reserves can now administer. The rights guaranteed by the Constitution have still not been clearly identified, and the government's promise of February 2018 to spell them out in a single law came to grief partly because the government remained in charge of the process, an example of lingering colonial attitudes.

Legislation has been passed to put First Nations in charge of child welfare, but it will almost certainly face difficulties being implemented. More accurate history is being written and taught, but the many negative myths about First Nations survive in the minds of too many Canadians, a dead weight to the momentum needed to address serious and expensive problems. Over half the population still believe Indigenous people should have no treaty rights (Angus Reid, June 2018).

So, what does the future hold? Canadian history since the 1830s clearly indicates that every attempt to assimilate First Nations and take away their treaty rights has failed. Given that record, their growing political strength and success since the Second World War, and their rapidly growing population and confidence, they are not going to "disappear." The policies that produced their poverty have been abandoned or are being changed, and that will continue to have a positive effect. So will the closing of the gap between government spending on Indigenous and non-Indigenous Canadians. Public pressure is building to address issues such as missing and murdered women, the high incarceration rates, the absence of First Nations on juries, the sterilization of women, or the continued adoption into non-Indigenous families. The meaning of "meaningful consultations" is slowly being clarified.

The sad history of the treatment of First Nations also reveals another example of the incredible luck Canadians have enjoyed in their corner of the world. First Nations are a remarkably honest and patient people, perhaps too honest and patient for their own good. They had every reason to join the Northwest Rebellion in 1885 as Ottawa was violating the treaties it had just signed and starving them into submission. But they signed in the presence of their Creator and would not break their word. There have been no Indian uprisings and remarkably little violence against their oppressors. Since Confederation they have resorted to appealing to politicians, to using the courts when allowed to do so, to mainly peaceful demonstrations, to some political activism. But patience is limited, as the Oka, Ipperwash and Gustafsen Lake incidents reveal, and governments and police are prone to mishandle such incidents as inquiries into these incidents also revealed. The Idle No More

Movement was a wake-up call but its not clear how many Canadians heard the alarm.

The policies and attitudes adopted by the current government and its achievements need to be pursued into the immediate future until politicians can say "promises fulfilled," until Canadians can say "problems solved," and until First Nations spokespersons can say "Thanks, about time." Then there will be equality between Indigenous and non-Indigenous Canadians, between all Canadian men and women, and Canadian colonialism will finally be a thing of the past. An Environics poll in July 2019 found that almost three-quarters of Indigenous youth are optimistic about reconciliation. Eighty-nine percent said it was important for non-Indigenous Canadians to understand their history. Hopefully that will be helped by books like "Understanding First Nations."

Bibliography:

In addition to numerous websites, over 1,000 newspaper and magazine articles were consulted, mainly from APTN, CBC, CTV, Global News, Macleans, the Globe and Mail, and the Ottawa Citizen. The list is available from the author at books@fromseatosea.com, 613-740-0895, or 2130 Dutton Crescent, Ottawa, ON, K1J 6K4.

SECONDARY SOURCES

Alcantara, Christopher. *Negotiating the deal: Comprehensive Land Claims in Canada.* Toronto: University of Toronto Press, 2013.

Asch, Michael. "Building Relations: Confederation, Treaties and Settler Obligations Today," in Ladner, Kiera L. and Myra J. Tait. *Surviving Canada: Indigenous Peoples Celebrate 150 Years of Betrayal.* Winnipeg: AARP Press, 2017.

Asch, Michael. *On Being Here to Stay: Treaties and Aboriginal Rights in Canada.* Toronto: University of Toronto Press, 2014.

Battiste, Marie and Jean Barman, eds. *First Nations Education in Canada: The Circle Unfolds*. Vancouver: University of British Columbia Press, 1995.

Belanger, Yale, ed., *Aboriginal Self-Government in Canada: Current Trends and Issues*. Saskatoon: Purich Publishing, 2008.

Belanger, Yale. *Ways of Knowing: an Introduction to Native Studies in Canada*. 3rd. ed. Toronto: Nelson, 2018.

Bland, Douglas. L. *Time Bomb: Canada and the First Nations*. Toronto: Dundurn Press, 2014.

Borrows, John. *Canada's Aboriginal Constitution.* Toronto: Toronto University Press, 2010.

Borrows, John. *Freedom and Indigenous Constitutionalism.* Toronto: University of Toronto Press, 2016.

Borrows, John and Michael Coyle, eds. *The Right Relationship: Reimagining the Implementation of Historical Treaties*. Toronto: University of Toronto Press, 2017.

Borrows, John. *Recovering Canada: the Resurgence of Indigenous Law.* Toronto: University of Toronto Press, 2007.

Canada's History Society. *Treaties and Treaty Relationships*. Winnipeg: Canada's History, 2018.

Cardinal, Harold. *The Unjust Society.* Edmonton: Hurtig, 1969.

Carleson, Nellie & Kathleen Steinhauer. *Disinherited Generations*. Edmonton: The University of Alberta Press, 2013.

Coates, Kenneth. *A Global History of Indigenous Peoples: Struggle and Survival.* Basingstoke, England: Palgrave Macmillan, 2004.

Coates, Kenneth. "Everyone needs to take a deep breath after the Trans Mountain ruling," in *Inside Policy*. Ottawa: September, 2018.

Coates, Kenneth. *#Idlenomore and the Remaking of Canada*. Regina: University of Regina Press, 2015.

Coulthard, Glen Sean. *Red Skin, White Masks: Rejecting the Colonial Politics of Recognition*. Minneapolis: University of Minnesota Press, 2014.

Crosby, Andrew and Jeffrey Monaghan. *Policing Indigenous Movements: Dissent and the Security State*. Winnipeg: Fernwood Publishing, 2018.

Crowley, Brian Lee. "Tearing down statues is not reconciliation," in *Inside Policy*. Ottawa: September, 2018.

Dashuk, James. *Clearing the Plains: Disease, Politics of Starvation and the Loss of Aboriginal Life.* Regina: Regina University Press, 2013.

Dickason, Olive. *Canada's First Nations: A History of Canada's Founding Peoples from Earliest Times*. Toronto: Oxford University Press, 1997.

Dubois, Janique and Kelly Saunders. "Unfinished Business: Bringing the Métis into Confederation," in Ladner, Kiera L. and Myra J. Tait. *Surviving Canada: Indigenous Peoples Celebrate 150 Years of Betrayal.* Winnipeg: AARP Press, 2017.

Ferrara, Nadia. *Reconciling and Dehumanizing Indigenous-settler Relations*. London: Lexington Books, 2015.

First Nations and Indigenous Studies, UBC. indigenousfoundations.arts.ubc.ca.

Flanagan, Tom, Christopher Alcantara, and André Le Dressay. *Beyond the Indian Act.* Montreal: Queens-McGill Press 2010.

Flanagan, Tom. *First Nations? Second Thoughts*. 2nd. ed. Montreal: McGill-Queen's Press, 2010.

Francis, Daniel. *The Imaginary Indian*. 2nd. ed. Vancouver: Arsenal Pulp Press, 2011.

Gale, Sharleen. "First Nations want access to capital, not handouts," in *Inside Policy*. Ottawa: September, 2018.

Gallagher, Bill. *Resource Rulers: Fortune and Folly on Canada's Road to Resources.* Self-published 2011.

George, Rachael Yacaal. "Inclusion is Just the Canadian Word for Assimilation: Self-Determination and the Reconciliation Paradigm in Canada," in Ladner, Kiera L. and Myra J. Tait. *Surviving Canada: Indigenous Peoples Celebrate 150 Years of Betrayal.* Winnipeg: AARP Press, 2017.

Harmon, Alexandra, ed. *The Power or Promises: Rethinking Indian Treaties in the Pacific Northwest.* Seattle: University of Washington Press, 2008.

Hedican, Edward. *Understanding Aboriginal Issues*. 2nd ed. Toronto: University of Toronto Press, 2008.

Henderson, James Youngblood. "O Canada: A Country cannot bc built on a living lie," in Ladner, Kiera L. and Myra J. Tait. *Surviving Canada: Indigenous Peoples Celebrate 150 Years of Betrayal.* Winnipeg: AARP Press, 2017.

Henderson Joseph, , James Youngblood. *Treaty Rights in the Constitution of Canada.* Toronto: Carswell, 2007.

Ivison, John. *Trudeau: The Education of a Prime Minister.* Toronto: Penguin, 2019.

Joseph, Bob. *21 Things You May Not Know About the Indian Act.* Vancouver: Indigenous Relations Press, 2018.

Joseph, Bob and Cynthia F. Joseph. *Indigenous Relations: Insights, Tips and Suggestions to Make Reconciliation a Reality.* Vancouver: Indigenous Relations Press, 2019

Joseph, Bob and Cynthia F. Joseph. *Working Effectively with Indigenous Peoples, 4th ed.* Vancouver: Indigenous Relations Press, 2017.

Kelm, Mary-Ellen and Keith D. Smith. *Talking Back to the Indian Act.* Toronto: University of Toronto Press, 2018.

King, Thomas. *The Inconvenient Indian: A Curious Account of Native Life in North America.* Toronto: Doubleday, 2012.

Ladner, Kiera L. "150 Years and Waiting: Will Canada Become an Honourable Nation?" in Ladner, Kiera L. and Myra J. Tait. *Surviving Canada: Indigenous Peoples Celebrate 150 Years of Betrayal.* Winnipeg: AARP Press, 2017.

Ladner, Kiera L. and Myra J. Tait. *Surviving Canada: Indigenous Peoples Celebrate 150 Years of Betrayal.* Winnipeg: AARP Press, 2017.

Lightfoot, Sheryl R. "Adopting and Implementing the United Nations Declaration on the Rights of Indigenous Peoples: Canada's Existential Crisis," in Ladner, Kiera L. and Myra J. Tait. *Surviving Canada: Indigenous Peoples Celebrate 150 Years of Betrayal.* Winnipeg: AARP Press, 2017.

Lightfoot, Sheryl. *Global Indigenous Politics: A Subtle Revolution.* New York: Routledge Press, 2016.

Lutz, John Sutton. *Makuk: A New History of Aboriginal-White Relations*. Vancouver: University of British Columbia Press, 2008.

Macdonald, David B. "Forgetting to Celebrate: Genocide and Social Amnesia as Foundational to the Canadian Settler State," in Ladner, Kiera L. and Myra J. Tait. *Surviving Canada: Indigenous Peoples Celebrate 150 Years of Betrayal.* Winnipeg: AARP Press, 2017.

Macdonald, David and Daniel Wilson. *Poverty or Prosperity: Indigenous Children in Canada.* Ottawa: Canadian Centre for Policy Alternatives, 2013.

Mandell, Louise. "We Will Help Each Other Be Great and Good," in Ladner, Kiera L. and Myra J. Tait. *Surviving Canada: Indigenous*

Peoples Celebrate 150 Years of Betrayal. Winnipeg: AARP Press, 2017.

Manuel, Arthur. *Unsettling Canada.* Toronto: Between the Lines Press, 2015.

McMillan, Alan D. *Native Peoples and Cultures of Canada.* 2nd. ed. rev. Toronto: Douglas & McIntyre, 1995.

Milward, David. "Reconciliation on Trial: Evaluating What Reconciliation Means in the Context of Aboriginal Justice," in Ladner, Kiera L. and Myra J. Tait. *Surviving Canada: Indigenous Peoples Celebrate 150 Years of Betrayal.* Winnipeg: AARP Press, 2017.

Miller, J.R. *Canada and the Aboriginal People 1867-1927.* Ottawa: Canadian Historical Society, 1997.

Miller, J.R. *Compact, Contract, Covenant: Aboriginal Treaty-Making in Canada.* Toronto: University of Toronto Press, 2009.

Miller, J.R. *Skyscrapers Hide the Heavens: A History of Indian-White Relations in Canada.* 4th ed. Toronto: University of Toronto Press, 2018.

Monchalin, Lisa. *The Colonial Problem: An Indigenous Perspective on Crime and Injustice in Canada*. Toronto: University of Toronto Press, 2016.

Palmater, Pamela. *Beyond Blood: Rethinking Indigenous Identity.* Saskatoon: Purich Publishing, 2011.

Palmater, Pamela. *Indigenous Nationhood: Empowering Grassroots Citizens*. Saskatoon: Fernwood Publishers, 2015.

Paul, Daniel. *First Nations History: We Were Not the Savages*. 3rd ed. Winnipeg: Fernwood Publishing, 2006.

Poplzer, Greg and Ken Coates. *From Treaty Peoples to Treaty Nations: a Road Map for Canada.* Vancouver: University of British Columbia Press, 2015.

Ray, Arthur J. "History Wars and treaty rights in Canada" in Harmon, Alexandra, ed. *The Power or Promises: Rethinking Indian Treaties in the Pacific Northwest.* Seattle: University of Washington Press, 2008.

Rose, Rupert. *Indigenous Healing: Exploring Traditional Paths*. Toronto: Penguin Group, 2014.

Russell, Peter. "Can Canada Retrieve the Principles of its First Confederation," in Ladner, Kiera L. and Myra J. Tait. *Surviving Canada: Indigenous Peoples Celebrate 150 Years of Betrayal.* Winnipeg: AARP Press, 2017.

Russell, Peter. *Canada's Odyssey: A Country Based on Incomplete Conquests.* Toronto: University of Toronto Press, 2017.

Sanna, Ellyn & William Hunter. *Canada's Modern-Day First Nations.* Philadelphia: Mason Crest Publishers, 2006.

Satzewich, Vic and Terry Wotherspoon. *First Nations: Race, Class, and Gender Relations*. Regina: Canadian Plains Research Centre, 2000.

Saul, John Ralston. *A Fair Country: Telling Truths About Canada*. Toronto: Viking Canada, 2008.

Sears, Robin V., "Indigenous Peoples' Health: Our Biggest Challenge to Reconciliation," *Policy*. Volume 6, Issue 3, Ottawa, 2018.

Sellars, Bev. *Price Paid: The Fight for First Nations Survival*. Vancouver: Talonbooks, 2016.

Sholts, Adam. *A History of Canada in Ten Maps*. Toronto: Allen Lane, 2017.

Symington, Fraser. *The Canadian Indian.* Toronto: McClelland & Stewart, 1969.

Tait, Myra L. "Kapyong and Treaty One First Nations," in Ladner, Kiera L. and Myra J. Tait. *Surviving Canada: Indigenous Peoples Celebrate 150 Years of Betrayal.* Winnipeg: AARP Press, 2017.

Talaga, Tanya. *Seven Fallen Feathers: Racism, Death, and Hard Truths in a Northern City*. Toronto: Anansi Press, 2017.

The Truth and Reconciliation Commission of Canada. *What We Have Learned: Principles of Truth and Reconciliation.* nd.

Vowel, Chelsea. *Indigenous Writes: A Guide to First Nations, Métis and Inuit Issues in Canada.* Winnipeg: Highwater Press, 2016.

Younging, Gregory. "Inherited History, International Law, and the UN Declaration." *Response, Responsibility, and Renewal: Canada's Truth and Reconciliation Journey*. Ottawa: Aboriginal Healing Foundation, 2007.

Younging, Gregory, Jonathan Dewar and Mike DeGagné, eds. *Response, Responsibility, and Renewal: Canada's Truth and Reconciliation Journey*. Ottawa: Aboriginal Healing Foundation, 2007.

Warry, Wayne. *Ending Denial: Understanding Aboriginal Issues*. Peterborough: Broadview Press, 2007.

Wherry, Aaron. *Promise and Peril: Justin Trudeau in Power*. Toronto, Harper Collins Publishers, 2019.

Wilson-Raybould, Jody. *From Where I Stand: Rebuilding Indigenous Nations for a Stronger Canada*. Vancouver: Purich, 2019.

Index

N

O

P

Q

R